BEYOND BORDERS

Winning Strategies for International Business

Discover the Key Principles Driving Business Development, Strategic Collaborations and Digital Transformation!

Vikram Anand

ACKNOWLEDGMENT

I would like to express my gratitude to mentors, colleagues, business leaders, and industry experts who have shared their wisdom and experiences over the years. Their insights have contributed immensely to my growth as a business development professional, and I hope to pass on the same value to readers through this book.

Table of Contents

Preface

What truly drives the business growth of an organization—having the best product or service, the most competitive pricing, or something far more strategic?

Business development is not just about closing deals; it is about creating long-term value, forging partnerships, and positioning an organization for sustained success in an ever-evolving market. In today's dynamic global economy, businesses that are thriving are not just those with great offerings, but those that can anticipate market shifts, leverage emerging technologies, navigate regulatory complexities, and build resilient networks of collaboration.

This book is the culmination of my two decades of experience in project management and business development across energy, infrastructure, and global markets. Throughout my career, I have had the opportunity to work in diverse environment, lead multi-million-dollar negotiations, manage crisis situations, and drive strategic expansions into new territories. These experiences have reinforced one undeniable truth: ***business development is as much about adaptability as it is about strategy***.

The inspiration for this book came from my own journey—from leading business expansion efforts in international markets to overcoming unforeseen crises such as the Ebola outbreak and the COVID-19 pandemic. Each challenge provided invaluable insights, and each success reinforced the power of strategic planning, resilience, and relationship-building.

What This Book Offers

This book is designed as a practical guide for business development professionals, executives, and entrepreneurs who are looking to master the complexities of growth, market expansion, and strategic partnerships. It is structured to offer:

> - **Actionable Strategies** – Proven frameworks for market entry, strategic alliances, and business expansion.
> - **Real-World Case Studies** – Insights from successful business development initiatives.
> - **Emerging Trends** – A forward-looking approach to how AI, sustainability, and digital transformation are reshaping business development.
> - **Practical Tools** – Business development templates, research methodologies, and industry glossaries for professionals to use in real-world applications.

This book is intended for the following community of professionals:

> - Aspiring business development professionals looking to build a strong foundation in market strategy, negotiation, and relationship management.
> - Industry executives and business leaders seeking insights on global expansion, risk mitigation, and strategic growth.

- ➢ Entrepreneurs and startup founders who need structured business development strategies to scale their ventures.
- ➢ Corporate decision-makers involved in mergers, acquisitions, and international trade negotiations.
- ➢ Students of Management who are interested to study real world case studies of international business dynamics

A Journey of Learning and Growth

Business development is not a short-term game but a long journey. The principles outlined in this book are not rigid rules but rather guiding frameworks that must evolve with market conditions, technological advancements, and business objectives.

I hope that the insights shared in this book serve as a resource and roadmap for professionals navigating the complex yet rewarding world of business development. Whether you are entering new markets, forging high-value partnerships, or overcoming unexpected challenges, may this book equip you with the knowledge, strategies, and mindset to drive sustainable business success.

Chapter 1: Introduction

Business development is often perceived as a function focused on sales and revenue generation, but in reality, it is a multifaceted discipline that requires a deep understanding of markets, strategic foresight, and the ability to build long-term relationships. In an increasingly interconnected world, where industries are evolving at an unprecedented pace, mastering business development is no longer optional—it is essential for survival and growth. Companies that thrive are those that anticipate market trends, align their capabilities with emerging opportunities, and execute well-crafted strategies that create sustainable competitive advantages.

Through my years of experience working across international markets, I have learned that business development is as much an art as it is a science. It involves not only data-driven decision-making but also the intuition to recognize untapped potential and the tenacity to navigate uncertainties. It is the art of creating long-term value for an organization through strategic planning, relationship building, and informed decision-making.

In today's rapidly evolving global economy, professionals must adapt to emerging trends, leverage technology, and navigate complex market dynamics to stay ahead of the competition.

The Purpose of this book

This book aims to serve as a comprehensive guide for business professionals, entrepreneurs, and executives seeking to master the intricacies of business development. By blending strategic insights with real-world case studies, it provides practical lessons on how to drive growth, overcome challenges, and capitalize on opportunities. Drawing from my extensive experience in international business development, particularly in the energy sector, this book will illuminate the principles, strategies, and tools necessary for achieving sustainable success in global markets.

Through this journey, we will explore business development strategies that have been tested in some of the world's most challenging environments, including high-stakes contract negotiations, project management under crisis conditions, and leveraging artificial intelligence for data-driven decision-making. Whether you are a seasoned professional or an aspiring business leader, the lessons shared in this book will equip you with the knowledge and skills to navigate the complexities of modern business landscapes.

Personal Journey in Business Development

My career in business development has been an exhilarating ride across continents, industries, and market cycles. Over two decades, I have had the privilege of working with leading global organizations, driving multi-million-dollar deals, and executing strategic growth initiatives in the oil and gas, energy, and consulting sectors. The journey has been defined by a commitment to excellence, an unrelenting pursuit of opportunities, and the ability to transform challenges into stepping stones for success.

Starting my career as an engineer in India's energy sector, I quickly realized that my passion lay beyond technical operations—I was drawn to the strategic and commercial aspects of the business. I wanted to be at the forefront of decision-making, influencing growth strategies and driving impactful business outcomes. This realization led me to transition into business development, where I learned the art of market entry, stakeholder engagement, and negotiation.

Throughout my career, I have navigated economic downturns, geopolitical challenges, and disruptive technological shifts. I have worked on high-profile projects, from negotiating the rehabilitation of the SAMIR Refinery in Morocco to leading the execution of a modular refinery project in Liberia. Each experience reinforced the importance of strategic foresight, adaptability, and resilience in the world of business development.

One of my most significant learnings has been the power of relationships—understanding that business development is not just about numbers, but about people. The ability to forge strong partnerships, build trust, and align interests with stakeholders is the true catalyst for long-term success. Whether dealing with multinational corporations, government bodies, or local enterprises, the human element remains central to every successful business development initiative.

The Role of Strategy in Sustainable Growth

Sustainable business growth does not happen by chance; it is the result of well-crafted strategies that align market opportunities with organizational capabilities. A strong strategy provides direction, minimizes risks, and ensures that every decision contributes to the long-term vision of the organization.

In today's business environment, the traditional approaches to growth are no longer sufficient. The rise of digital transformation, globalization, and artificial intelligence has redefined the way businesses operate. Companies must adopt agile strategies that leverage data-driven insights, innovative technologies, and collaborative partnerships to remain competitive.

The strategies outlined in this book are not theoretical constructs but tested methodologies that have been applied in real-world business scenarios. They cover a broad spectrum of business development aspects, including:

- **Market Research and Feasibility Analysis** – Understanding market trends, competitive landscapes, and customer needs before making investment decisions.
- **Stakeholder Engagement and Negotiation** – Building strong relationships and structuring deals that create mutual value.
- **Technology and AI in Business Development** – Harnessing the power of artificial intelligence to

drive smarter decision-making and optimize business operations.

> **Crisis Management and Resilience** – Navigating economic uncertainties, geopolitical shifts, and unforeseen crises with strategic agility.
> **Operational Efficiency and Cost Optimization** – Identifying ways to enhance efficiency, reduce costs, and improve bottom-line performance.

By understanding and implementing these strategies, businesses can achieve sustainable growth and long-term profitability in even the most challenging environments.

As we embark on this journey together, I encourage you to approach business development not just as a function but as a mindset—a dynamic and proactive approach to creating value. The stories, case studies, and insights shared in this book are designed to inspire, challenge, and empower you to become a more strategic and successful business development professional.

Let's begin this journey of discovery, strategy, and successful outcomes.

Chapter 2: Foundations of Business Development

Business development is the backbone of any organization's growth strategy. It serves as the bridge between an organization's vision and its market reality, requiring a blend of analytical thinking, creativity, and relationship management. Successful business development professionals do not merely react to market changes; they anticipate shifts, create opportunities, and build sustainable revenue streams. This foundational understanding is what separates thriving businesses from those struggling to stay relevant.

In this chapter, we will delve into the essential components of business development—understanding its lifecycle, key skills and traits required for success, and the evolving challenges and opportunities in the global energy market.

A well-structured business development framework ensures that companies do not rely solely on reactive measures but proactively cultivate opportunities. By developing an in-depth understanding of the business development lifecycle, professionals can build resilient strategies that withstand economic fluctuations, industry disruptions, and competitive pressures. Whether you are an industry veteran with years of experience or a newcomer looking to establish your foothold, grasping these fundamentals will provide a solid framework for advancing in business development vertical and setting yourself apart in an increasingly dynamic business landscape.

Understanding the Business Development Lifecycle

Business development is not a one-time event but a continuous process that follows a structured lifecycle. It involves identifying opportunities, cultivating relationships, and executing strategies that lead to sustainable growth. The business development lifecycle provides a roadmap that ensures companies to systematically expand their reach, mitigate risks, and achieve long-term success. Understanding this cycle allows professionals to anticipate challenges, optimize decision-making, and stay ahead of competitors.

⇒ **Key Stages of the Business Development Lifecycle are as follows:**

1. **Market Research and Opportunity Identification**

   Every strategic business development initiative begins with thorough research. This stage involves analyzing market trends, understanding customer needs, assessing competition, and identifying gaps that can be transformed into growth opportunities. Organizations leverage data analytics, industry reports, and emerging technologies like AI to derive actionable insights that form the foundation for future strategies.

2. **Lead Generation and Prospecting**

Once opportunities are identified, the next step is to generate leads—potential clients, partners, or investors who align with the business's objectives. This process involves targeted networking, leveraging digital platforms, attending industry events, and establishing brand visibility through content marketing. Building a strong pipeline of prospects ensures a steady influx of potential business opportunities.

3. **Relationship Building and Stakeholder Engagement**

Business development is fundamentally about relationships. Establishing trust and credibility with stakeholders is crucial for long-term success. Effective communication, understanding client pain points, and offering tailored solutions strengthen business relationships. Personalizing interactions and demonstrating genuine value proposition help convert prospects into long-term partners.

4. **Deal Structuring and Negotiation**

This phase requires a strategic approach to structuring agreements that are mutually beneficial. Strong negotiation skills, a deep understanding of financial implications, and legal acumen play a vital role in closing deals. Transparency, flexibility, and the ability to navigate complex discussions contribute to successful deal-making and long-term commitments.

5. **Execution and Delivery**

Winning a deal is only half the battle; ensuring its successful execution is where true value is realized. This phase involves project management, resource allocation, performance monitoring, and meeting client expectations. Maintaining consistency, efficiency, and adaptability in delivering promised solutions reinforces a company's reputation and increases the likelihood of repeat business.

6. **Growth and Expansion**

Once an initial deal is successfully executed, business development does not stop—it evolves into nurturing ongoing partnerships, exploring additional opportunities, and expanding into new markets. Companies that continuously refine their strategies and seek diversification achieve long-term sustainable growth. Monitoring industry shifts and adapting to changing market conditions ensure continued growth.

By mastering the business development lifecycle, professionals can navigate complex market landscapes, drive consistent growth, and create long-term value for their organizations.

Let's explore the key skills and traits that define a successful business development leader and how they contribute to sustained success.

Key Skills and Traits of a Successful Business Development Leader

Business development leaders require a unique blend of skills and personal attributes to navigate complex markets and drive growth. As a business development professional, one must possess the ability to think strategically, communicate effectively, negotiate persuasively, and adapt quickly to ever-changing business environments. Success in this field requires not only technical expertise but also strong interpersonal and leadership capabilities.

Some of the key skills required to be a successful business development leader are as follows:

1. **Strategic Thinking**

   Business development leaders must have a visionary mindset, identifying long-term opportunities and aligning them with the company's goals. They need to anticipate market trends, assess risks, and develop strategies that ensure sustainable growth. The ability to think ahead and proactively create opportunities rather than react to circumstances is a defining trait of successful business development professionals.

2. **Effective Communication**

   Clear and persuasive communication is at the heart of business development. Leaders must be able to articulate value propositions, engage stakeholders, and present compelling business cases. Whether negotiating with clients, engaging with internal teams, or delivering presentations to investors, strong communication skills are essential for influencing decisions.

3. Negotiation and Persuasion

The ability to negotiate effectively is a crucial skill in business development. Leaders must strike a balance between maximizing value for their organization while ensuring that deals remain attractive to clients and partners. This requires an understanding of human psychology, business acumen, and a structured approach to negotiations to achieve win-win outcomes.

4. Adaptability and Resilience

The business landscape is constantly evolving, and market conditions can shift unpredictably. Successful business development professionals embrace change, remain agile in their approach, and find ways to navigate obstacles. Resilience is critical in overcoming setbacks and maintaining focus on long-term goals despite short-term challenges.

5. Networking and Relationship Management

Building and maintaining strong professional relationships is a cornerstone of business development. Leaders must cultivate networks within their industry, nurture client relationships, and develop partnerships that lead to long-term success. The ability to engage meaningfully with diverse stakeholders fosters trust and opens doors to new opportunities.

6. **Data-Driven Decision Making**

Modern business development relies heavily on data analysis. Leaders must be able to interpret market research, financial reports, and competitive intelligence to make informed decisions. The integration of AI and big data analytics enhances their ability to identify trends, evaluate risks, and optimize business strategies.

By mastering these skills and traits, business development professionals can enhance their effectiveness, drive revenue growth, and ensure long-term success for their organizations.

Challenges and Opportunities in the Global Market

Given my extensive experience in the energy sector, spanning my entire career; I am particularly interested in sharing my perspective about this sector.

The global energy market is a dynamic and evolving industry that presents both significant challenges and promising opportunities. Business development professionals in this sector must navigate regulatory frameworks, economic fluctuations, and technological disruptions while identifying and capitalizing on emerging trends.

⇒ **Key Challenges in the Energy Sector are as follows:**

1. **Fluctuating Oil Prices**

   The energy industry is highly volatile, with oil and gas prices experiencing frequent fluctuations due to geopolitical tensions, supply-demand imbalances, and macroeconomic factors. Business development leaders must develop strategies to mitigate the impact of price instability on long-term investments.

2. **Regulatory and Compliance Hurdles**

   Governments worldwide impose strict regulations on energy production, environmental compliance, and safety standards. Navigating these regulatory landscapes requires an in-depth understanding of international policies and the ability to adapt business models to ensure compliance while maintaining profitability.

3. **Geopolitical Risks**

   Energy markets are influenced by global political dynamics, trade policies, and conflicts. Business leaders must anticipate geopolitical shifts, assess risks, and develop contingency plans to safeguard operations and investments.

4. **Transition to Renewable Energy**

   The growing emphasis on sustainability and decarbonization is transforming the energy sector. Companies that fail to adapt to the increasing demand for clean energy solutions risk becoming obsolete. Business development leaders must proactively explore opportunities in renewable energy, carbon capture technologies, and energy efficiency solutions.

Likewise, there are several opportunities for Growth and Innovation in the energy sector as follows:

1. **Emerging Markets and Infrastructure Development**

   Rapid industrialization in developing countries presents opportunities for expanding energy infrastructure. There are multiple potential opportunities available to be explored in areas such as refineries, power plants, and renewable energy in Africa, Asia, and Latin America.

2. **Technological Advancements in Energy Production**

   Innovations in artificial intelligence, automation, and energy storage are transforming the industry. Companies that leverage these technologies to optimize operations and reduce costs will gain a competitive advantage in the market.

3. **Sustainable Energy Investments**

   Governments and investors worldwide are increasingly focusing on renewable energy initiatives. Business development leaders who align their strategies with sustainability goals can secure funding, form strategic partnerships, and capitalize on the growing clean energy market opportunities.

4. **Strategic Partnerships and Mergers**

Collaborations between energy companies, technology firms, and financial institutions are opening new revenue streams. Forming alliances with key stakeholders enhances market positioning and fosters innovation-driven growth.

Similarly, business development professionals with a deep insight about their industry are well-positioned to understand and navigate the global business landscape.

By analyzing your respective sector-specific challenges and opportunities, you can develop resilient strategies, adapt to market shifts, and drive long-term business growth.

Chapter 3: Strategic Planning and Market Entry

Strategic planning is an integral part of business development for an organization. It provides the roadmap for an organization's market entry, expansion, and long-term sustainability. Without a clear strategy, companies risk making haphazard decisions that lead to inefficiencies and missed opportunities. A well-defined strategic plan enables businesses to assess potential markets, analyze competition, and align their resources to achieve optimal growth.

Market entry, on the other hand, is one of the most critical stages of business development. Expanding into new markets presents both immense opportunities and significant challenges. Whether entering a domestic or international market, organizations must conduct thorough research, adapt to local regulations, and establish competitive advantages. The success of market entry depends on a company's ability to anticipate barriers, build strong relationships, and leverage innovative tools with AI to gain strategic insights.

Case Study: Expansion of SAGA's Global Business Post-COVID

The COVID-19 pandemic disrupted economies and business operations worldwide, forcing companies to reassess their strategies, streamline their operations, and adopt innovative approaches to maintain growth. My

Company i.e SAGA Global Consultants (referred to as SAGA), specializing in engineering consultancy and project management in the energy sector, faced significant challenges during this period but emerged stronger through strategic decision-making and an adaptive approach to market expansion.

⇒ **Challenges Faced by SAGA Post-COVID**

1. **Decline in Global Investment** – The pandemic led to a downturn in global investments in energy projects, causing project delays and cancellations. Many companies, including SAGA's clients, tightened their budgets and prioritized essential operations over expansion initiatives.
2. **Travel and Operational Restrictions** – With borders closed and travel restrictions in place, traditional methods of business development, such as in-person negotiations and site visits, were no longer viable.
3. **Workforce and Supply Chain Disruptions** – Project execution was hindered by labor shortages, supply chain bottlenecks, and fluctuating raw material costs.

⇒ **Strategic Response and Business Expansion**

Despite these challenges, our business development team at SAGA leveraged a proactive approach, focusing on adaptability, digital transformation, and strategic partnerships to drive its global expansion post-pandemic. The key strategic moves included:

1. **Digital Transformation and AI Integration**

> SAGA team adopted digital platforms for client engagement, virtual negotiations, and project management.

2. **Diversification into New Geographies and Services**

> Recognizing shifts in global energy investments, SAGA strategized to expand its presence into key African markets with growing energy infrastructure demand.
> We diversified our service portfolio, offering feasibility studies, asset optimization, and advisory on conventional as well as sustainable energy investments.

3. **Strengthening Client Relationships and Strategic Partnerships**

> SAGA prioritized strengthening existing client relationships, offering tailored consulting services that aligned with post-pandemic recovery plans.
> Forming strategic alliances with regional partners allowed SAGA to navigate local regulations, build trust, and expand its reach.

4. **Operational Efficiency and Cost Optimization**

> A thorough review of internal processes led to cost-saving measures, increasing operational efficiency.
> The company adopted remote collaboration tools to reduce overhead

costs and improve communication among international teams.

Results and Impact

The strategic actions taken by SAGA during and post-COVID times resulted in remarkable business growth:

> A **150% increase in global business revenue** within two years.
> Successful **entry into new international markets** with active projects.
> Strengthened relationships with major energy corporations, leading to long-term contracts and repeat business.

The expansion of SAGA Global Consultants serves as a testament to the power of strategic planning, adaptability, and leveraging technology to overcome crises. The company management's ability to pivot quickly and embrace innovative approaches enabled it not only to survive but to thrive in the post-pandemic era.

Blueprint for Market Research and Strategic Planning for Business Development

Strategic market research and planning serve as the foundation for successful business development. Without a clear understanding of market dynamics, customer needs, and competitive landscapes, companies risk making uninformed decisions that hinder their growth. A well-structured approach to market research enables businesses to identify viable opportunities, assess risks, and develop strategies that align with their long-term objectives. The key steps to implement such an approach are as follows:

Step 1: Identifying Market Opportunities

The first step in business development is recognizing where opportunities exist. This involves:

- Analyzing macroeconomic trends and industry shifts.
- Understanding customer pain points and unmet needs.
- Evaluating regulatory frameworks and compliance requirements.
- Studying emerging markets with high growth potential.

By leveraging data analytics and AI-driven insights, companies can pinpoint lucrative segments and tailor their approach to maximize impact.

Step 2: Competitive Analysis and Benchmarking

Understanding the competitive landscape is critical in developing a robust market entry strategy. This includes:

- Identifying key competitors and their market positioning.
- Analyzing competitor strengths, weaknesses, opportunities, and threats (SWOT analysis).
- Benchmarking pricing models, service offerings, and customer engagement strategies.
- Assessing gaps in the market that provide a competitive edge.

Step 3: Defining Market Entry Strategy

Once a market is selected, the next step is crafting a tailored entry strategy. Key considerations include:

> Choosing between organic growth, partnerships, acquisitions, or joint ventures.
> Determining the optimal business model for the new market (B2B, B2C, franchising, licensing, etc.).
> Establishing a local presence through strategic alliances.
> Developing a pricing and value proposition that resonates with target customers.

Step 4: Financial and Risk Assessment

Every business expansion involves financial investment and inherent risks. A detailed feasibility analysis ensures:

> Projected revenue and profitability align with company goals.
> Key risks, including geopolitical, financial, and operational, are identified in advance and suitably mitigated.
> A sustainable budget for market penetration is in place.
> Funding sources, partnerships, and investment options are evaluated.

Step 5: Implementation and Execution

Even the most well-designed strategy must be executed effectively. This involves:

- ➢ Establishing a local operational team or working with channel partners.
- ➢ Implementing robust marketing and sales strategies.
- ➢ Monitoring key performance indicators (KPIs) to track success.
- ➢ Adjusting strategies based on market feedback and real-time data.

The success of this approach highlights how technology can enhance strategic decision-making, mitigate risks, and drive business growth.

Utilizing Generative AI for Strategic Insights

Artificial Intelligence (AI) has revolutionized the way businesses conduct market research, develop strategies, and execute business development initiatives. Generative AI, in particular, is reshaping the strategic landscape by offering deep insights derived from vast datasets, automating decision-making processes, and generating predictive analytics that enhance business growth strategies.

Generative AI can be leveraged to enhance Strategic Planning to support business development in the following ways:

1. **Data-Driven Market Research**

   - ➢ Generative AI enables businesses to analyze vast amounts of structured and unstructured data from various sources, including industry

reports, competitor strategies, and consumer behavior trends.
- ➢ AI-powered tools provide real-time insights into emerging market trends, allowing businesses to make informed strategic decisions.

2. Competitive Intelligence and Forecasting

- ➢ Businesses can leverage AI models to track competitor activities, pricing trends, and customer sentiments.
- ➢ Predictive trends and analytics can help in forecasting demand, pricing fluctuations, and market disruptions, enabling companies to stay ahead of the competition.

3. Personalized Customer Engagement

- ➢ AI-driven systems can tailor marketing messages and sales strategies to specific customer segments based on behavioral analytics.
- ➢ Chatbots and virtual assistants powered by AI can improve customer interactions, offering personalized recommendations and support.

4. Optimizing Business Development Processes

- ➢ AI programs can be utilized to automate repetitive tasks such as lead scoring, contract analysis, and market segmentation, allowing business development teams to focus on high-value strategic activities.

> Generative AI tools can help to generate detailed reports, proposals, and presentations, accelerating decision-making processes.

5. **Risk Assessment and Scenario Planning**

> AI-driven simulations allow businesses to evaluate various market entry scenarios, assessing potential risks and outcomes.
> By analyzing historical data and economic indicators, AI can help in mitigating risks and identifying the most viable business expansion strategies.

Real-World Application: AI-Driven Expansion Strategies

The Business Development team at SAGA has successfully implementing AI-driven strategies during our post-COVID business expansion initiatives. By integrating Generative AI tools with the traditional business development methods, we have been able to achieve the following outcomes:

> Real-time competitive analysis across multiple global markets.
> Identified untapped business opportunities using AI-powered market intelligence platforms.
> Developed AI-assisted proposals that reduced turnaround time for contract negotiations.
> Automated client engagement processes, improving conversion rates and client retention.

The Future of AI in Business Development

As AI technology continues to evolve, businesses that embrace Generative AI will gain a competitive edge in strategic planning and market entry. The integration of AI-driven insights with human expertise will define the future of business development, fostering more accurate decision-making, efficient operations, and sustainable growth.

By utilizing Generative AI, companies can optimize market research, enhance business intelligence, and execute more precise, data-backed strategies. The combination of human intuition and AI-driven insights creates a powerful synergy that enables organizations to navigate the complexities of modern business landscapes effectively.

Chapter 4: Negotiation and Relationship Building

Negotiation and relationship building are at the core of successful business development. In today's highly competitive and interconnected global markets, securing business deals is not just about numbers—it is about trust, credibility, and long-term value creation. While a strong business strategy and competitive pricing play an important. role, the ability to negotiate effectively and foster meaningful relationships can determine whether a deal is won or lost.

A well-executed negotiation is not just about getting the best deal in the short term; it is about crafting agreements that are mutually beneficial, ensuring all parties involved see value in the collaboration. Similarly, strong relationships with stakeholders—clients, partners, investors, and regulators—create the foundation for sustained growth and business expansion. The best business development professionals recognize that while a single contract can bring in revenue, lasting relationships pave the way for continued success. This chapter delves into the art of negotiation, the strategies behind high-stakes deal-making, and the principles of long-term relationship management, with real-world insights drawn from experience.

Case Study: Securing the Service Contract for Cabinda Refinery in Angola

In the competitive landscape of the global energy sector, winning a high-value contract requires a blend of strategic negotiation, deep market understanding, and strong stakeholder engagement. One such instance was the successful negotiation of a service contract for the Cabinda Refinery project in Angola, a deal that showcased the importance of patience, adaptability, and value-driven communication in high-stakes business development.

The Challenge: A Competitive and Complex Negotiation Landscape

The Cabinda Refinery project, led by **Gemcorp Holdings UK**, is a significant modular refinery initiative aimed at enhancing Angola's domestic refining capacity. Securing a role in this project was complex and required significant efforts. Several well-established engineering firms were vying for contracts, and the competition was intense. The key challenges faced during the negotiation process included:

1. **Fierce Competition** – Major international firms were also bidding for contracts, requiring a differentiated approach to stand out.
2. **Complex Organizational Hierarchies** – The negotiation process involved multiple stakeholders, including government agencies, investors, and project consultants, each with their own interests and expectations.
3. **Strategic Pricing Concerns** – Balancing a competitive pricing structure while ensuring

profitability and long-term value creation was crucial.

4. **Trust and Relationship-Building** – With the shareholders of this project being highly relationship-driven, earning trust and credibility was essential for securing the contract.

The Approach: A Negotiation Strategy Rooted in Value and Trust

To navigate these challenges and secure the contract, a multi-layered negotiation strategy was employed as follows:

1. **Leveraging Past Success & Industry Credibility**

   - A strong case was built based on prior successful projects, particularly the Conex Petroleum Refinery project in Liberia.
   - Demonstrating a proven track record of delivering high-quality engineering and consultancy services reinforced our credibility.

2. **Customized Value Proposition**

   - Instead of offering generic services, the proposal was tailored to meet the specific operational needs of the Cabinda Refinery.
   - The contract scope was expanded to include engineering documentation, operator training, pre-commissioning, commissioning, and O&M support for the Refinery to provide a one-stop solution.

3. **Navigating the Negotiation Process with a Relationship-First Approach**

   ➤ Extensive one-on-one discussions were held with key decision-makers to understand their specific pain points and long-term project vision.
   ➤ Flexibility in contract structuring allowed for a win-win solutions, ensuring both parties felt confident in the negotiation process.

4. **Strategic Pricing & Risk Mitigation**

   ➤ While keeping the bid competitive, risk-sharing mechanisms were introduced to align incentives and minimize financial exposure for both parties.
   ➤ Performance-based clauses were included to guarantee long-term project success.

The Outcome: A Landmark Contract Secured

Through a well-calculated negotiation approach, the service contract was successfully secured with Gemcorp Holdings UK which is a major shareholder of the Cabinda Oil Refinery project. The contract terms ensured not only immediate project involvement but also a strategic foothold for future expansion in the Angolan energy sector.

Here are the noteworthy takeaways from the negotiation process:

   ➤ **Building trust is as crucial as offering competitive pricing.** Without credibility and

stakeholder confidence, price alone cannot win a
deal.

> **Tailoring the value proposition** to address
  client-specific needs increases the likelihood of
  success.
> **Negotiation is a long game.** A patient and
  strategic approach to building relationships often
  pays off more than aggressive bidding.
> **Risk-sharing enhances contract security.**
  Structuring agreements to align interests ensures
  long-term commitment from both parties.

This case study exemplifies how negotiation is not just
about financial terms—it's about relationships,
adaptability, and long-term strategic thinking. In the next
section, we will explore the principles of effective
negotiation in high-stakes deals, drawing from industry's
best practices and real-world applications.

Principles of Effective Negotiation in High-Stakes Deals

Negotiation in business development, particularly in
high-stakes deals, is both an art and a science. It requires
a blend of strategic preparation, psychological insight,
and tactical execution to secure agreements that are
beneficial to all parties involved. In high-value contracts,
where millions of dollars and long-term partnerships are
at stake, mastering the principles of negotiation can mean
the difference between success and failure. Below are the
key principles that drive successful negotiations in
complex business environments.

1. Preparation is Everything

A well-prepared negotiator is a confident negotiator. Before entering discussions, thorough research must be conducted to understand:

- The needs and priorities of the other party.
- The financial, operational, and strategic implications of the deal.
- Market trends, competitor offers, and alternative solutions.
- Possible objections and counterarguments.

Being armed with data ensures that the negotiator is well-positioned to counter objections and present a compelling case that aligns with the counterpart's objectives.

2. Establishing Trust and Credibility

High-stakes deals are rarely transactional—they are built on trust. Clients, investors, and partners need to be confident that the business delivering the solution is credible, reliable, and committed to long-term success. Building trust involves:

- Demonstrating industry expertise and a track record of success.
- Being transparent about the scope, risks, and expectations.
- Maintaining consistent and professional communication throughout the process.

Trust transforms negotiations from adversarial to collaborative problem-solving.

3. The Power of Value Over Price

While pricing plays a crucial role in negotiations, it is not the only determinant of a successful deal. Clients are often more concerned about the value they receive than just the cost. Successful negotiators:

> Shift the discussion from price to long-term value creation.
> Highlight unique differentiators—such as service quality, expertise, efficiency, and risk mitigation.
> Offer additional strategic benefits, such as after-sales support, operational consulting, or technology integration.

Focusing on value rather than cost helps negotiators avoid price wars and strengthen their position.

4. Strategic Concessions and Win-Win Solutions

A skilled negotiator understands that not all terms are deal-breakers. Instead of rigidly pushing a single agenda, the focus should be on creating a win-win outcome by:

> Identifying areas of flexibility where concessions can be made.
> Offering alternative solutions that address both parties' needs.
> Structuring creative trade-offs that allow both sides to gain something valuable.

A negotiator who is open to compromise but firm on core objectives can craft deals that satisfy both parties.

5. Controlling the Pace and Managing Emotions

High-stakes negotiations can be intense, involving multiple stakeholders with conflicting interests. The ability to control the pace of discussions and manage emotions are key to maintaining a strong position. Successful negotiators:

> Remain patient and avoid rushing into decisions due to pressure.
> Use silence as a strategic tool, allowing the other party to reveal more information.
> Stay calm and composed, even when faced with aggressive tactics or high-pressure moments.

Emotional intelligence is just as crucial as business intelligence in turning difficult negotiations into successful deals.

6. Negotiation Leverage: Understanding Your Strengths

Every negotiation involves leverage—factors that give one party an advantage over the other. Recognizing and utilizing leverage strategically can help tip the balance in one's favor. Leverage can come from:

> A strong industry reputation and successful past projects.
> Scarcity of alternatives—if the negotiator offers a unique solution unavailable elsewhere.
> A proven financial and operational track record that mitigates client risk.
> Exclusive partnerships or proprietary technology that adds unique value.

By identifying key leverage points, negotiators can confidently steer discussions toward favorable terms.

7. The Power of Silence and Listening

One of the most overlooked yet powerful negotiation tactics is active listening. Rather than dominating the conversation, successful negotiators:

> Listen carefully to the other party's concerns, goals, and objections.
> Ask strategic questions that encourage the other side to reveal their priorities.
> Use silence effectively to create space for reflection and decision-making.

The best negotiators talk less and listen more, allowing them to craft responses that directly address the counterpart's needs.

8. Risk Mitigation and Contingency Planning

No high-stakes deal comes without risks, whether financial, operational, or legal. Strong negotiators anticipate potential risks and proactively include safeguards in their contracts, such as:

> Performance-based clauses that ensure accountability.
> Exit strategies and dispute resolution mechanisms to handle unforeseen challenges.
> Clear definitions of scope, deliverables, and timelines to avoid ambiguities.

Having well-structured contingency plans instills confidence in all stakeholders and strengthens mutual credibility.

9. Closing with Confidence and Clarity

Once a deal nears completion, securing a strong close is critical. A successful close requires:

> ➢ Summarizing agreed-upon terms clearly to ensure alignment.
> ➢ Ensuring both parties are confident about the terms before signing of the contract.
> ➢ Expressing enthusiasm and reinforcing the mutual benefits of the partnership.

A strong and decisive close cement the deal and lays the groundwork for future collaborations.

Applying These Principles in High-Stakes Deals

These principles were integral to securing the service contract for the Cabinda Refinery, where trust-building, strategic concessions, and a value-driven approach played a key role. By mastering these principles, business development professionals can consistently win negotiations and build enduring partnerships.

Building Long-Term Relationships with Stakeholders

In business development, securing a contract is only the beginning; sustaining and growing relationships with stakeholders is what truly ensures long-term success. Whether dealing with clients, investors, government entities, or business partners, the ability to build and nurture relationships is a key differentiator between transactional success and lasting industry influence. Stakeholders who trust a company and its leadership are far more likely to engage in repeat business, refer new opportunities, and collaborate on future ventures.

It's important to remind ourselves that strong stakeholder relationships are not built overnight. They require consistent engagement, reliability, transparency, and the ability to add value beyond the immediate business transaction. The following strategies outline the core principles for developing and maintaining long-term stakeholder relationships.

1. Establishing Trust and Credibility from the Beginning

Trust is the foundation of every strong business relationship. Without it, even the most lucrative contracts can unravel. To establish and maintain credibility, business leaders must:

> - **Deliver on commitments** consistently—meeting deadlines, providing quality service, and ensuring reliability.
> - **Maintain transparency** in communications, whether about project progress, challenges, or financial matters.
> - **Act with integrity**, always prioritizing ethical business practices.

Building trust takes time, but once established, it becomes a powerful asset in business negotiations and partnership development.

2. Maintaining Open and Proactive Communication

Effective stakeholder engagement relies on clear, open, and regular communication. This means not just keeping stakeholders informed, but also proactively engaging with them to understand their evolving needs and expectations. Best practices include:

> **Regular check-ins and updates** on projects, industry developments, or new opportunities.
> **Active listening** to stakeholder concerns and addressing them with solutions.
> **Personalized engagement**, ensuring that communication is tailored to the needs of different stakeholders.

Consistent and meaningful communication keeps relationships strong, even during challenging business cycles.

3. Providing Continuous Value Beyond the Deal

Long-term relationships thrive when stakeholders see ongoing value beyond the initial business transaction. This can be achieved by:

> **Offering industry insights and market intelligence** that help stakeholders make better business decisions.
> **Providing strategic guidance** even when there's no immediate deal in place.
> **Facilitating introductions and networking opportunities**, connecting stakeholders with valuable business partners.

By remaining a valuable resource, business leaders position themselves as indispensable partners, ensuring long-term loyalty.

4. Navigating Challenges with a Relationship-First Approach

Challenges and disagreements are inevitable in business, but how they are managed can define the strength of a stakeholder relationship. A **relationship-first approach** to problem-solving includes:

> - **Addressing conflicts promptly and constructively**, seeking win-win solutions rather than getting caught in the blame game.
> - **Being flexible and accommodating** when circumstances require adjustments to agreements.
> - **Ensuring fairness in all business dealings**, even when tough decisions must be made.

Stakeholders appreciate companies that are responsive, fair, and solution-oriented, strengthening long-term loyalty.

5. Investing in Long-Term Partnerships

Successful business relationships are not short-term engagements—they are strategic alliances that evolve over time. Companies that prioritize long-term collaboration over one-time gains benefit from:

> - **Repeat business opportunities** with familiar and trusted partners.
> - **Stronger industry influence and reputation** within key markets.
> - **Higher referral rates**, as satisfied stakeholders recommend services to others.

Treating each business relationship as an investment in future growth leads to sustainable success.

6. Adapting to Stakeholder Needs and Industry Shifts

Markets evolve, and so do stakeholder needs. Businesses that continuously adapt and innovate maintain stronger relationships by:

> - **Staying ahead of industry trends** and sharing insights with stakeholders.
> - **Evolving service offerings** to match changing business requirements.
> - **Investing in new technologies and capabilities** to enhance stakeholder partnerships.

Flexibility and adaptability ensure that relationships remain relevant and valuable over time.

Final Thoughts: The Power of Relationship-Driven Business Development

While securing contracts is an essential component of business development, the real strength of a company lies in its ability to cultivate and sustain meaningful relationships. By focusing on trust, continuous engagement, and long-term value creation, businesses can ensure lasting partnerships, repeat business, and industry leadership.

Effective relationship-driven business development goes beyond transactions; it involves continuous engagement, understanding client needs, and providing solutions that drive their success. This is where the role of Business Development professionals, as the key interface with the Client organizations become crucial. By staying connected, anticipating challenges, and supporting clients through market shifts, they can position their businesses not only as service providers but as trusted advisors and strategic collaborators.

Moreover, enduring relationships often become gateways to new opportunities, including referrals, joint ventures, and strategic alliances, which are invaluable for business growth. Companies that prioritize relationship-building over short-term gains are more likely to achieve industry leadership, client loyalty, and sustainable success in competitive markets.

In essence, while deals may drive revenue, it is relationships that drive lasting business growth and industry influence.

Chapter 5: Techno-Commercial Evaluations and Cost Optimization

In business development, particularly within capital-intensive industries like energy, refining, and infrastructure, decision-making is not solely based on market potential or financial projections. Instead, it requires a thorough techno-commercial evaluation—a balanced assessment of both the technical feasibility and commercial viability of a project. This evaluation ensures that investments are not only technically sound but also financially sustainable, providing long-term value to stakeholders while optimizing costs.

Cost optimization, on the other hand, plays a critical role in enhancing the profitability and competitiveness of projects. Effective cost management goes beyond simple budget-cutting; it involves identifying inefficiencies, leveraging innovative solutions, and negotiating strategic contracts that align with long-term business goals. Business development professionals must be adept at evaluating technical proposals, understanding financial implications, and aligning project strategies with market realities. This chapter will explore the principles of techno-commercial evaluations and cost optimization, beginning with a real-world case study on the rehabilitation of the SAMIR Refinery in Morocco—a project where strategic cost evaluation played a pivotal role in the investment decision about the refinery's future.

Case Study: Techno-Commercial Evaluation for the Rehabilitation Project of SAMIR Refinery in Morocco

Background:

The SAMIR Refinery, once the backbone of Morocco's petroleum industry, had been non-operational since 2015 due to financial and operational challenges. As the country's sole refinery, its closure led to increased reliance on fuel imports, raising national energy costs and supply chain risks. Several stakeholders, including potential investors, policymakers, and industry leaders, saw the potential in reviving the refinery—but the challenge lay in conducting a comprehensive techno-commercial evaluation to determine whether rehabilitation was a viable and financially justifiable option.

The Challenge: A Complex, High-Stakes Project

Bringing the SAMIR Refinery back to operational status required a multi-faceted evaluation process. Several hurdles had to be addressed:

1. **Aging Infrastructure and Technical Viability**

   - The refinery had been dormant for years, raising concerns about equipment degradation, outdated technology, and potential safety risks.
   - A thorough technical assessment was required to evaluate the feasibility of upgrading existing infrastructure versus replacing critical components.

2. **Regulatory and Environmental Compliance**

   ➢ Restarting operations meant aligning with modern day environmental regulations, emissions control standards, and sustainability measures.
   ➢ Compliance with Morocco's evolving energy policies and global best practices was crucial for securing government approvals.

3. **Financial Viability and Cost Optimization**

   ➢ A major concern for potential investors was whether the rehabilitation investment could deliver sustainable returns.
   ➢ Given the global shift towards renewable energy, assessing the refinery's competitiveness in a changing energy market was crucial.

4. **Market Demand and Strategic Positioning**

   ➢ The feasibility study had to determine whether the local and regional demand for refined petroleum products justified the refinery's revival.
   ➢ Alternative scenarios, including partial revamping for specialized fuel production, were also explored.

The Approach: A Comprehensive Techno-Commercial Evaluation

To address these challenges, a structured evaluation framework was deployed by our Team, involving technical specialists, financial analysts, and market strategists. The key steps included:

1. Technical Feasibility Assessment

> - On-site inspections and audits were conducted to evaluate the structural integrity of key assets, including distillation units, catalytic reformers, and storage tanks.
> - Advanced predictive maintenance tools and digital simulations were used to estimate repair costs versus new investments.
> - A comparative analysis of different rehabilitation scenarios (full restoration vs. modular revamp) was carried out.

2. Cost Optimization and Financial Modeling

> - A cost-benefit analysis was undertaken to determine the most economical approach to rehabilitation.
> - Operational cost reductions were identified through process automation, digital refinery solutions, and supply chain optimization.
> - Multiple funding models were assessed, including public-private partnerships (PPPs) and phased investment strategies to reduce upfront capital expenditure.

3. Market Demand and Revenue Forecasting

- A detailed supply-demand analysis was conducted to assess long-term market needs for refined petroleum products in Morocco and neighboring regions.
- Competitive pricing strategies were explored, ensuring the refinery's output remained profitable against global market fluctuations.
- Risk assessments were carried out to account for geopolitical, economic, and regulatory uncertainties.

The Outcome: A Data-Driven Roadmap for Refinery Rehabilitation

The evaluation revealed that a phased rehabilitation approach—where essential infrastructure would be restored first, followed by modular upgrades—offered the best balance between cost efficiency and long-term operational viability.

Key results from the study were:

- A 10% reduction in estimated project revamp costs (approx. $30 million in savings) through optimized procurement and energy-efficient technology.
- A projected Internal Rate of Return (IRR) of 15%, making the investment financially viable for stakeholders.
- A reduced payback period of 8-10 years, enhancing investor confidence.
- Government and stakeholder alignment, leading to early-stage funding commitments.

This case study highlights how strategic techno-commercial evaluations help businesses make informed decisions, mitigate risks, and optimize costs in large-scale infrastructure projects. In the next section, we will break down the fundamental principles of techno-commercial evaluations and cost optimization for business development professionals.

Understanding Techno-Commercial Evaluations and Cost Optimization as a Business Development Professional

In high-stakes business development, particularly in industries like oil & gas, infrastructure, and manufacturing, investment decisions must be made with a balance of technical feasibility and commercial viability. This is where techno-commercial evaluations play a crucial role. Business development professionals must develop the ability to assess projects not just from a sales or operational standpoint but from an integrated strategic perspective, ensuring that projects are both financially viable and technically sustainable.

Cost optimization is an essential aspect of this process, as it enables companies to maximize value while minimizing inefficiencies. In today's competitive landscape, simply securing a contract is not enough—ensuring cost-effective execution and long-term profitability is what differentiates successful businesses. This section delves into the fundamental principles of techno-commercial evaluations and cost optimization, equipping business development professionals with insights on how to make informed investment and execution decisions.

1. What does Techno-Commercial Evaluation mean?

A techno-commercial evaluation is a structured process that assesses a business opportunity from both technical and commercial perspectives to determine its feasibility, risks, and financial implications. It answers the following key questions:

> **Technical Feasibility:** Can the project be executed with the available technology, resources, and infrastructure?
> **Commercial Viability:** Does the project make financial sense? Will it generate sustainable revenue and return on investment?
> **Risk Assessment:** What are the potential risks (operational, financial, regulatory) and how can they be mitigated?

A well-executed techno-commercial evaluation reduces uncertainties, prevents cost overruns, and ensures that investments are made strategically.

2. The Key Components of a Techno-Commercial Evaluation

A. Technical Feasibility Analysis

> Assessing the current state of assets, infrastructure, and operational capacity.
> Evaluating required upgrades, modifications, or new technology implementations.

➢ Identifying potential technical bottlenecks that could delay project execution.
➢ Ensuring regulatory and environmental compliance with industry standards.

B. Financial and Commercial Viability

➢ Cost estimation and capital expenditure (CAPEX) analysis—assessing how much investment is required.
➢ Operational expenditure (OPEX) assessment—forecasting long-term costs for maintenance, labor, and utilities.
➢ Revenue forecasting—analyzing potential earnings based on market demand and competitive pricing.
➢ Break-even analysis and payback period calculations—determining how soon the project will become profitable.

C. Market and Risk Analysis

➢ Evaluating supply-demand dynamics and competitive positioning.
➢ Identifying key market drivers and disruptors that could impact financial returns.
➢ Performing risk analysis (financial, geopolitical, technological) and developing mitigation strategies.

3. The Role of Cost Optimization in Business Development

Cost optimization is not just about cutting expenses—it is about improving efficiency and maximizing value. Smart cost optimization strategies ensure that projects remain financially attractive while maintaining high standards of execution.

Key techniques of cost optimization include:

A. Strategic Procurement and Vendor Negotiations

> - Leveraging bulk purchasing and long-term supplier contracts to reduce costs.
> - Identifying alternative suppliers that offer better pricing or quality.
> - Ensuring supply chain efficiency to avoid cost overruns and delays.

B. Process Automation and Digitalization

> - Implementing AI-driven analytics to track project performance and identify inefficiencies.
> - Utilizing predictive maintenance tools to reduce downtime and repair costs.
> - Streamlining operations with digital solutions like cloud-based project management.

C. Energy and Resource Efficiency

> - Incorporating energy-saving technologies to lower operating costs.
> - Reducing material waste through improved supply chain optimization.

> Identifying alternative fuel and renewable energy sources for cost-effective operations.

D. Financial Engineering and Investment Structuring

> Exploring public-private partnerships (PPPs) and structured financing to minimize upfront costs.
> Implementing performance-based contracts that align costs with outcomes.
> Using hedging strategies to mitigate currency fluctuations and commodity price risks.

4. How Business Development Professionals Can Apply These Principles

For business development professionals, mastering techno-commercial evaluations and cost optimization strategies provides a competitive edge as follows:

> **Enhancing Proposal Competitiveness** – Understanding cost structures allows for **smarter bidding** and improved proposal pricing strategies.
> **Stronger Stakeholder Negotiations** – Business leaders who understand both the **technical and commercial** aspects of a project gain more credibility with investors and decision-makers.
> **Risk-Informed Decision-Making** – Having a holistic view of potential technical and

financial risks ensures better planning and execution.

> **Driving Long-Term Profitability** – Smart cost optimization strategies ensure higher returns and project sustainability.

Final Thoughts: Balancing Technology, Finance, and Strategy

Techno-commercial evaluations and cost optimization are fundamental pillars of strategic business development. Whether launching or revamping an industrial project, or investing in new infrastructure, the ability to assess technical feasibility while ensuring commercial success is a game-changer.

As industries evolve, business development professionals must continuously refine their ability to evaluate projects, optimize costs, and align strategic decisions with market realities. Mastering these skills ensures that every project undertaken is not only technically sound but also financially rewarding, driving sustainable business growth.

Risk Mitigation Strategies in Business Development

In business development, every decision comes with a degree of risk—whether financial, operational, technological, or geopolitical. While some risks are inevitable, how they are managed determines the success or failure of a project. Effective risk mitigation strategies allow organizations to anticipate potential challenges, minimize financial exposure, and safeguard business interests. This is especially critical in industries like oil & gas, infrastructure, and large-scale investments, where high capital expenditure and long project timelines amplify risks.

A structured approach to risk management ensures that businesses remain resilient in the face of uncertainties. This section explores key risk categories and the most effective strategies for identifying, assessing, and mitigating risks in business development.

1. Identifying Key Risks in Business Development

Understanding risks is the first step toward managing them effectively. Business development professionals must assess risks across multiple dimensions:

A. Financial and Investment Risks

> - **Market Volatility** – Fluctuations in product/commodity prices, interest rates, or foreign exchange rates can impact project profitability.
> - **Funding Risks** – Delays or limitations in securing investment capital can stall project execution.
> - **Liquidity Risks** – Poor cash flow management may lead to financial instability.

B. Operational and Technical Risks

- ➢ **Project Delays** – Infrastructure bottlenecks, supply chain disruptions, or unforeseen site conditions can impact timelines.
- ➢ **Technology Risks** – Implementing new or unproven technology carries risks of failure, inefficiency, or obsolescence.
- ➢ **Workforce Challenges** – Shortages in skilled labor, union disputes, or regulatory compliance issues can affect execution.

C. Geopolitical and Regulatory Risks

- ➢ **Government Policy Shifts** – Sudden changes in taxation, tariffs, or industry regulations can impact financial models.
- ➢ **Trade Restrictions & Sanctions** – Political instability or diplomatic tensions may limit market access.
- ➢ **Environmental Compliance Risks** – Stricter environmental laws can lead to additional compliance costs or project redesigns.

D. Market and Competitive Risks

- ➢ **Demand Fluctuations** – Miscalculating market demand can lead to underutilization of assets or financial losses.
- ➢ **Competitive Threats** – Emerging market players or disruptive technologies may reduce market share.

➢ **Supplier and Vendor Risks** – Dependence on a few key suppliers can lead to disruptions if they fail to deliver.

2. Strategies for Risk Mitigation

Risk mitigation requires proactive planning, scenario analysis, and strategic adaptability. Below are some of the most effective approaches for managing risks in business development:

A. Financial Risk Mitigation

➢ **Hedging Strategies** – Using financial instruments like futures contracts to protect against commodity price fluctuations.

➢ **Diversified Revenue Streams** – Avoiding over-reliance on a single client, market, or funding source.

➢ **Phased Investments** – Breaking large projects into phases to reduce upfront financial exposure.

B. Operational Risk Mitigation

➢ **Robust Project Management** – Implementing standardized process frameworks to minimize execution risks.

➢ **Supply Chain Resilience** – Identifying backup suppliers and alternative logistics routes to avoid bottlenecks.

- ➢ **Technology Validation** – Conducting rigorous pilot testing and scenario simulations before full-scale deployment.

C. Geopolitical and Regulatory Risk Mitigation

- ➢ **Engagement with Government & Policy Advocates** – Maintaining close collaboration with regulatory authorities to stay ahead of policy changes.
- ➢ **Local Partnerships & Compliance Programs** – Forming alliances with regional players who understand the local regulatory landscape.
- ➢ **Risk Monitoring Systems** – Using AI-driven analytics to track geopolitical events and predict potential disruptions.

D. Market and Competitive Risk Mitigation

- ➢ **Agile Business Models** – Ensuring adaptability by diversifying product/service offerings.
- ➢ **Customer-Centric Approach** – Conducting frequent market research and demand analysis to stay aligned with consumer needs.
- ➢ **Competitor Benchmarking** – Constantly assessing competitor strategies to stay ahead in the market.

Final Thoughts: Integrating Risk Management into Business Development

Risk is an inherent part of business, but when managed correctly, it becomes an opportunity rather than a threat. By embedding structured risk assessment and mitigation strategies into business development processes, organizations can:

> - Improve project financial stability and investor confidence.
> - Avoid costly delays and operational inefficiencies.
> - Maintain regulatory compliance and protect investments.
> - Build resilient business models that thrive in dynamic market conditions.

Successful business leaders do not eliminate risk—they manage and leverage it strategically to drive competitive advantage. As industries continue to evolve on the landscapes of global business dynamics, business development professionals who are able to identify and manage risks effectively will remain at the forefront of sustainable and profitable growth.

Chapter 6: Leveraging Technology for Competitive Advantage

In today's rapidly evolving business landscape, technology is no longer a luxury but a necessity for maintaining a competitive edge. Companies that harness the power of today's technology viz. artificial intelligence (AI), big data, automation, and digital tools are better positioned to make informed decisions, optimize operations, and drive sustainable growth. The integration of technology in business development has revolutionized the way market research is conducted, deals are structured, and risks are assessed. From AI-powered analytics that predict market trends to digital platforms that streamline negotiations, the ability to leverage technology effectively can make the difference between industry leaders and underperformers.

For industries such as oil & gas, energy, and infrastructure, where investment decisions carry high stakes, the ability to process large datasets and derive meaningful insights is critical to strategic planning. The energy sector, in particular, is undergoing a major transformation, driven by advancements in digital technologies, automation, and sustainability-focused innovations.

This chapter explores how modern businesses can leverage AI and digital tools to enhance decision-making, improve efficiency, and stay ahead of industry disruptions. It begins with a real-world case study demonstrating how an AI-driven feasibility study transformed investment decision-making for a Fujairah oil terminal project, followed by a broader discussion on the role of AI in business development and emerging trends in the energy sector.

Case Study: AI-Driven Feasibility Study for Fujairah Oil Terminal

The global oil and gas industry is becoming increasingly complex, with market fluctuations, geopolitical uncertainties, and evolving energy policies influencing investment decisions. In this landscape, data-driven decision-making is paramount to mitigating risks and optimizing returns. One such example is the AI-driven feasibility study conducted for an oil storage terminal project in Fujairah, UAE, where artificial intelligence played a pivotal role in evaluating project viability, minimizing risks, and optimizing financial modeling.

The Challenge: A High-Risk Investment in a Competitive Market

Fujairah is a major energy hub, strategically located along key international shipping routes and serving as a crucial refueling and storage center. However, investing in a new oil storage terminal required a comprehensive feasibility study to assess the following parameters:

1. **Market Demand & Competitive Landscape**

   - Determining whether there is a strong business case for additional storage capacity in a region with multiple existing terminals.

> Understanding price trends, demand-supply projections, and regulatory factors affecting profitability.

2. Financial Viability & Risk Assessment

> Analyzing expected return on investment (ROI), internal rate of return (IRR), and capital expenditure (CAPEX) required for the project.

> Assessing geopolitical risks, oil price volatility, and potential regulatory hurdles.

3. Operational Optimization & Technology Integration

> Evaluating the most cost-effective design and automation solutions for storage, inventory management, and distribution.

> Leveraging AI-based predictive maintenance models to improve operational efficiency and reduce downtime.

The AI-Powered Approach to Feasibility Analysis

To navigate these complexities, advanced AI-driven analytics and big data models were utilized to generate a data-backed feasibility study, covering the following key aspects:

1. AI-Powered Market Intelligence and Demand Forecasting

- Big data analytics aggregated vast amounts of historical trading data, supply chain dynamics, and geopolitical trends to predict market fluctuations.
- AI forecasting models assessed future oil storage demands, allowing for a more accurate projection of capacity utilization and revenue generation.
- Competitor benchmarking was performed using machine learning algorithms, identifying gaps in service offerings and pricing inefficiencies.

2. Financial Modeling & Risk Mitigation Strategies

- AI-driven simulations modeled various financial scenarios, analyzing ROI under different market conditions.
- Risk assessment tools identified potential regulatory and geopolitical risks, providing real-time contingency planning recommendations.
- Data analyses from the AI tools helped us to arrive at the most cost-efficient procurement strategies, reducing overall project expenses by 8%.

3. Optimizing Operational Efficiency

> AI-integrated strategies helped us to arrive at optimized logistics and supply chain operations.
> Identification of critical assets helped us to strategize over minimizing potential equipment failures and downtime.

The Outcome: A Data-Backed Investment Strategy

As a result of AI-driven feasibility analysis, the project would potentially benefit from:

> A well-informed investment decision, with projected IRR of 22.38% and a payback period of 9 years, enhancing investor confidence.
> An optimized cost structure, with AI-driven cost savings of $15M across procurement and operational efficiencies.
> A reduced risk profile, with data-backed mitigation strategies incorporated into the business plan.
> Strong regulatory compliance, as AI simulations ensured alignment with evolving UAE energy policies.

This case study exemplifies how AI-driven decision-making enhances strategic planning, mitigates risks, and drives financial viability in large-scale infrastructure projects. In the next section, we will explore how AI and digital tools are revolutionizing modern business development, offering key insights into emerging technologies shaping the future of competitive advantage.

The Role of AI and Digital Tools in Modern Business Development

In today's digital age, artificial intelligence (AI) and digital tools have become indispensable for businesses looking to gain a competitive edge. No longer confined to just automating routine processes, AI is now shaping strategic decision-making, market intelligence, and operational efficiency. The ability to process vast amounts of data, derive actionable insights, and predict future trends has transformed business development into data-driven discipline.

For industries like oil & gas, energy, and infrastructure, where market fluctuations, regulatory shifts, and geopolitical uncertainties can impact business growth, AI-driven insights offer greater agility, reduced risks, and smarter investment strategies. Some of the key ways by which AI and digital tools are revolutionizing modern business development are highlighted below:

1. AI-Driven Market Research and Competitive Intelligence

Traditional market research methods—relying on historical trends, expert opinions, and manual analysis—are now being replaced by AI-powered solutions that offer real-time, predictive insights.

> **Big Data Analytics** – AI can process vast amounts of structured and unstructured data to identify emerging trends, pricing movements, and competitor strategies.

- ➢ **Predictive Market Modeling** – Machine learning algorithms can be used to forecast demand shifts, geopolitical risks, and investment opportunities, allowing businesses to make preemptive strategic moves.
- ➢ **Sentiment Analysis** – AI-driven sentiment tools can be leveraged to analyze social media, news reports, and industry discussions to gauge market perception and investor confidence.

A good example of its application can be: AI-powered analytics can be employed to predict fluctuations in global crude oil demand, enabling companies to optimize trading strategies and procurement decisions in response to future price shifts.

2. Automation in Business Development & Sales Processes

AI-driven automation is redefining lead generation, sales forecasting, and contract management in business development. By reducing manual inefficiencies, AI allows teams to focus on strategy rather than routine tasks.

- ➢ **AI-Driven Lead Generation** – AI tools can help analyze customer behavior, industry patterns, and past interactions to identify high-potential leads automatically.
- ➢ **CRM & Relationship Management** – AI-powered CRM platforms can be used to track stakeholder interactions, automate follow-ups,

and personalize communication, enhancing long-term engagement.

➢ **Contract Analysis & Risk Assessment** – AI tools can scan legal documents to identify risks, pricing inconsistencies, and compliance requirements, reducing negotiation timelines.

A good example of its application can be: Using AI-driven CRM solutions to improve conversion rates by personalizing client interactions based on behavioral insights.

3. AI-Powered Financial Modeling and Investment Decision-Making

Accurate financial forecasting is crucial for business expansion and investment planning. AI brings unprecedented precision to financial modeling by analyzing multiple economic indicators, pricing trends, and capital allocation scenarios.

➢ **AI-Based Risk Modeling** – AI can assess credit risks, market exposure, and financial stability, allowing companies to structure deals with reduced uncertainty.

➢ **Dynamic Pricing Models** – AI-driven algorithms can be implemented to adjust pricing structures based on real-time demand-supply fluctuations, ensuring maximum profitability.

➢ **Automated Investment Analysis** – AI can be used to evaluate financial reports, balance sheets, and revenue models to determine the most profitable business opportunities.

A good example of its application can be: Use of AI-powered financial modeling to help investors identify the best market entry points for renewable energy projects, optimizing capital allocation.

4. Smart Infrastructure and Operational Efficiency

For asset-heavy industries like energy, logistics, and manufacturing, AI-equipped infrastructure management solutions can be leveraged to optimize costs, performance, and risk mitigation.

> **Predictive Maintenance** – AI-powered sensors can analyze equipment performance in real time, reducing unplanned downtime and repair costs.
> **Supply Chain Optimization** – AI algorithms can identify inefficiencies in logistics and procurement, reducing costs while ensuring optimal inventory levels.
> **Energy Efficiency & Sustainability** – AI-driven energy management systems can help optimize fuel consumption and reduce environmental impact, enhancing ESG (Environmental, Social, and Governance) compliance.

A good example of its application can be: AI-driven predictive maintenance solutions in oil refineries can reduce unexpected shutdowns by as much as 40%, saving millions of dollars in lost revenue.

5. Cybersecurity & Risk Management in Business Development

As businesses adopt digital transformation, cybersecurity risks also increase proportionately. AI can play key role in detecting threats, preventing fraud, and securing critical data.

> **AI-Based Threat Detection** – AI can help to identify anomalies and potential cyberattacks before they impact business operations.
> **Automated Compliance Monitoring** – Integrated AI systems can be used to ensure regulatory compliance by monitoring evolving laws and industry standards in real time.
> **Fraud Prevention in Financial Transactions** – AI can help detect irregular patterns in transactions, preventing fraud and financial losses.

A good example of its application can be: AI-powered fraud detection can save companies millions in financial losses by identifying and protecting from suspicious activities.

6. The Integration of AI with Emerging Technologies

AI is not an isolated tool—it integrates with other cutting-edge technologies to unlock even greater potential in business development.

> **AI & Blockchain** – AI-powered blockchain solutions enhances transparency in supply chain and contract execution, reducing disputes.

- ➢ **AI & IoT (Internet of Things)** – Smart IoT sensors collect and process real-time operational data, improving efficiency in manufacturing and logistics.
- ➢ **AI & Cloud Computing** – AI-based cloud analytics enables seamless data sharing across global operations, enhancing decision-making speed.

A good example of its application can be: AI-IoT integration in automated logistics hubs improves supply chain efficiency by reducing costs and delays.

Thus, the integration of AI with big data, automation, and emerging technologies will redefine how businesses expand into new markets, manage risks, and create value. The ability to leverage AI effectively is not just an advantage—it is a necessity for business leaders looking to thrive in an era of digital transformation. Companies that embrace AI-driven decision-making, automation, and predictive analytics are well-positioned to stay ahead of market shifts, optimize costs, and secure long-term growth.

Future Trends in Technology and Their Implications for the Energy Sector

The energy sector is undergoing one of the most transformative periods in history, driven by digitalization, automation, artificial intelligence (AI), and sustainability-focused innovations. As the world moves towards decarbonization, efficiency optimization, and enhanced resource management, the role of technology in shaping the future of energy cannot be overstated. Companies that embrace emerging technologies will not only remain competitive but will also be at the forefront of industry-wide disruption and innovation.

From AI-driven energy forecasting to blockchain-enabled smart contracts, new technologies are redefining how businesses operate, manage risks, and make strategic decisions. This section explores key future trends and their long-term implications for the energy sector.

1. Artificial Intelligence (AI) and Machine Learning in Energy Optimization

AI is already transforming how energy businesses analyze market trends, optimize supply chains, and enhance operational efficiency. Looking forward, AI will play an even greater role in:

> - **Smart Grid Management** – AI-powered grids will self-regulate power distribution, optimizing supply and reducing energy waste.
> - **Predictive Energy Demand Forecasting** – AI will analyze weather patterns, economic indicators, and consumer behavior to predict energy consumption needs in real-time.
> - **Autonomous Decision-Making in Energy Trading** – AI-driven trading algorithms will optimize the buying and selling of energy, reducing price volatility and enhancing profitability.

Anticipated implication: AI will significantly reduce operational costs and improve energy allocation efficiency, making renewable energy integration more seamless.

2. Blockchain for Transparency and Decentralization in Energy Markets

Blockchain technology is revolutionizing how energy transactions are recorded and managed, enabling transparent, decentralized, and tamper-proof systems. The energy sector will immensely benefit from the following envisaged developments:

- **Smart Contracts for Power Purchase Agreements (PPAs)** – Automated contracts will enable seamless transactions between energy producers and buyers, reducing legal complexities.
- **Decentralized Energy Trading Platforms** – Consumers and businesses will trade excess energy peer-to-peer (P2P) without the need for intermediaries.
- **Carbon Credit and Emissions Tracking** – Blockchain will create verifiable carbon credit markets, ensuring transparency in emissions reductions.

Anticipated implication: Blockchain will reduce transaction costs, eliminate inefficiencies, and democratize energy distribution.

3. The Rise of Digital Twins in Asset Management

A digital twin is a virtual replica of physical energy assets that enables real-time monitoring, predictive maintenance, and performance optimization. Future applications would include:

> **Digital Twin Monitoring of Oil Refineries and Power Plants** – AI-enabled digital twins will simulate different operational scenarios, predicting failures before they happen.
> **Smart City Energy Management** – Urban planners will use digital twins to optimize energy efficiency across cities and industrial zones.
> **Enhanced Workforce Training** – Energy companies will use digital twins in VR-based training simulations for workforce safety and operational expertise.

Anticipated implication: Digital twins will extend asset lifespans, reduce maintenance costs, and enhance efficiency in large-scale energy operations.

4. Robotics and Automation in Energy Infrastructure

Automation and robotics are set to revolutionize refinery operations, offshore drilling, and grid maintenance. Future developments are likely to include:

> **Autonomous Drones for Pipeline and Offshore Monitoring** – AI-powered drones will conduct inspections, detect leaks, and prevent system failures without human intervention.

➢ **Self-Healing Grids** – Smart energy networks will automatically detect and correct faults, reducing downtime and improving power reliability.

➢ **Automated Refinery Operations** – Robotics will enhance hazardous energy production environments, improving safety and efficiency.

Anticipated implication: Robotics will reduce labor costs, enhance workplace safety, and minimize human error in complex energy operations.

5. Hydrogen and Renewable Energy Innovations

With the global push towards net-zero emissions, hydrogen and advanced renewables will reshape the energy mix. Some of the key envisaged innovations are:

➢ **Green Hydrogen Production via AI-Optimized Electrolysis** – AI will enhance the efficiency of hydrogen fuel production, making it a viable alternative to fossil fuels.

➢ **Solar and Wind Energy Optimization with AI** – AI-powered forecasting will maximize renewable energy yield by adjusting to climate conditions in real-time.

➢ **Next-Generation Battery Storage Solutions** – AI and machine learning will optimize battery performance, extending lifespan and increasing energy storage capabilities.

Anticipated implication: AI-driven energy solutions will accelerate the transition to renewables, reducing reliance on fossil fuels and lowering carbon emissions.

6. Edge Computing and IoT for Real-Time Decision Making

The future of energy will rely heavily on IoT-enabled edge computing, which will allow data to be processed closer to the source. This will lead to:

> **Real-Time Energy Monitoring** – IoT sensors in grids, plants, and refineries will provide **instant data analysis, improving efficiency and response times**.
> **AI-Optimized Demand Response** – Automated adjustments to energy production and consumption will help balance supply-demand fluctuations.
> **Grid Resilience and Cybersecurity** – Edge computing will reduce vulnerability to cyberattacks by decentralizing data processing.

Anticipated implication: Edge computing will increase energy system resilience, improve efficiency, and enable ultra-fast decision-making.

Final Thoughts: The Future of Tech-Driven Energy Business Development

Technology will continue to reshape the energy industry, making businesses more agile, cost-efficient, and environmentally sustainable. Companies that invest in AI, blockchain, digital twins, automation, and renewable innovations will lead the market, while those that fail to adapt will be at risk of falling behind.

The energy leaders of tomorrow will be those who embrace digital transformation today. As the industry moves toward decentralization, sustainability, and AI-driven efficiency, businesses must proactively adopt, integrate, and innovate with these technologies to maintain long-term competitiveness.

Chapter 7: Crisis Management and Innovative Approaches to Business Development

The ability to navigate crises is one of the defining traits of a resilient and forward-thinking business leader. Unforeseen challenges—be it a pandemic, economic downturn, geopolitical unrest, or industry disruption—can threaten business continuity, disrupt operations, and test the adaptability of organizations. However, businesses that embrace innovation, leverage first-principles thinking, and proactively manage risks are often able to emerge stronger from crises rather than being crippled by them.

In business development, crisis management is not just about damage control—it is about turning adversity into opportunity. Whether it is ensuring operational continuity during crises situation or executing high-stakes projects, leaders must apply strategic agility, technological innovation, and problem-solving frameworks to overcome challenges. This chapter explores real-world case studies and the principles of crisis management, demonstrating not just survival, but growth in business in the face of adversity.

Case Study: Transforming Training Business Through Virtual Solutions to Drive Business Continuity During COVID-19

The COVID-19 pandemic disrupted businesses worldwide, forcing organizations to rethink traditional models, accelerate digital transformation, and find innovative ways to sustain their business. Among the many industries affected, corporate training and professional development faced one of the biggest challenges. Travel restrictions, lockdowns, and social distancing requirements rendered instructor-led training (ILT) programs unviable, threatening business continuity for training service providers.

In response to these challenges, we at SAGA Global Consultants took a bold and innovative approach, successfully transforming our training business from a conventional ILT (i.e. Instructor Led Training) model to a Virtual Instructor-Led Training (VILT) model. This strategic move ensured that the company could continue delivering high-quality training services while expanding its client base and improving profitability.

The Challenge: A Sudden Halt to Traditional Training Methods

Prior to the pandemic, SAGA's training model was heavily reliant on in-person, classroom-based training sessions. With COVID-19 restrictions in place, the following key challenges emerged:

1. **Disruption of Business Operations** – The inability to conduct physical training sessions

meant an immediate halt to revenue-generating activities.

2. **Client Retention Issues** – Existing clients, accustomed to ILT sessions, were hesitant to shift to online training models.

3. **Training Quality and Engagement** – A major concern was ensuring that a virtual training model maintained the same level of interactivity, effectiveness, and knowledge retention as in-person training.

4. **Trainer Availability and Technology Adoption** – Trainers had to be retrained on virtual platforms, and infrastructure had to be set up to support online sessions seamlessly.

The Solution: Adopting a Virtual Training Model

Faced with these challenges, a strategic crisis management approach was implemented, using a combination of technology, first-principles thinking, and innovative learning methodologies:

1. Redesigning the Training Delivery Model

> **Shift from ILT to VILT** – A new Virtual Instructor-Led Training (VILT) model was introduced, allowing training sessions to be conducted entirely online.

> **Implementation of Learning Management System (LMS)** – A dedicated LMS platform was developed to host training content, assessments, and learner progress tracking.

> **Multimodal Learning** – The program integrated live virtual classes, self-paced modules, interactive case studies, group discussions, and online assessments to ensure high engagement and learning retention.

2. Engaging with Clients and Addressing their concerns

> **Personalized Consultations** – Clients were individually engaged to explain the benefits of VILT, demonstrating how it could match or even exceed the effectiveness of ILT.

> **Pilot Training Sessions** – Complimentary demo sessions were conducted to familiarize clients with the virtual model, addressing any concerns and collecting feedback for improvements.

> **Flexible Training Schedules** – Online training allowed for greater flexibility, with sessions designed to accommodate different time zones and individual learning paces.

3. Upskilling Trainers and Technology Adoption

> **Trainer Enablement Programs** – Internal trainers were equipped with necessary skils to leverage online training tools, including virtual whiteboards, breakout rooms, and interactive Q&A platforms to maintain engagement levels.

> **AI-Powered Learning Analytics** – Data-driven insights were used to track learners' progress, engagement levels, and knowledge retention,

allowing for real-time improvements in course delivery.

> **Seamless Digital Experience** – High-quality video conferencing platforms, AI-driven chatbots for learner support, and cloud-based resources ensured a smooth and professional training experience.

The Outcome: A Profitable and Scalable Training Model

> **Business Continuity Maintained** – The transition to virtual training ensured zero revenue loss, allowing SAGA to retain its client base and sustain our business throughout the pandemic.

> **Expansion to New Markets** – The VILT model removed geographic barriers, enabling SAGA to acquire new clients across multiple regions, expanding our business reach.

> **Improved Profitability** – By eliminating travel and venue costs, operational expenses were reduced, leading to higher profit margins compared to in-person training.

> **Higher Client Satisfaction** – Feedback from clients indicated strong acceptance of the new model, with many choosing to continue virtual training even after restrictions were lifted.

Key Takeaways from the Crisis Response

> Digital transformation is not just about survival—it's about future-proofing the business.

> Client engagement and education are critical when introducing new solutions.
> A crisis can be an opportunity to innovate, differentiate, and scale operations.

This case study highlights how adaptive thinking, technology integration, and strategic crisis management can turn business challenges into opportunities for long-term growth.

In the next section, we will explore Lessons from managing projects during the Ebola Crisis, where crisis leadership was applied in high-stakes, real-world scenarios.

Lessons from Managing Projects During the Ebola Crisis in West Africa

Crises test the resilience, adaptability, and problem-solving skills of business leaders. Whether dealing with a global pandemic or a regional outbreak, ensuring project continuity in uncertain times requires a combination of strategic foresight, operational flexibility, and proactive risk management. The **Ebola outbreak in West Africa (2014–2016)** posed significant challenges for businesses operating in that region. However, businesses that leveraged innovative problem-solving approaches were able to maintain continuity, minimize disruptions, and emerge stronger.

This section examines key lessons in crisis management drawn from real-world experiences, particularly the $15M Conex Petroleum Storage Terminal Construction Project in Liberia during the Ebola crisis. This case study provides valuable insights into how business development leaders can navigate crises while ensuring operational efficiency and financial sustainability.

Lesson 1: Crisis Resilience Begins with Strong Project Leadership

During the Ebola outbreak in Liberia, the $15M Conex Petroleum Storage Terminal Construction Project was at risk of severe disruptions, with:

- **Severe travel and workforce restrictions**, limiting on-site operations.
- **Logistical challenges**, including supply chain delays and material shortages.
- **Health and safety concerns**, requiring immediate preventive efforts to protect workers.

Despite these challenges, the project was successfully completed on schedule and under budget, with a $2M cost savings. The key success factor was proactive leadership that anticipated challenges and implemented contingency plans.

Thus, the lesson here is: Leading through crises requires a structured approach, including:

- ➢ Preemptive risk identification and mitigation planning.
- ➢ Strong stakeholder communication to align on expectations and adaptations.
- ➢ A leadership team that remains calm, decisive, and solutions-driven under pressure.

Lesson 2: Risk Mitigation Requires Strong Stakeholder Collaboration

During the Ebola crisis, effective risk mitigation strategies ensured that the Conex Petroleum Storage Terminal project was delivered despite severe regional disruptions. The approach included:

- ➢ **Collaborating with local authorities** to ensure compliance with evolving health and safety regulations.
- ➢ **Engaging alternative suppliers** to mitigate supply chain disruptions.
- ➢ **Implementing enhanced workforce safety protocols**, including PPE distribution and medical check-ups.

Thus, the lesson here is: Building strong relationships with local authorities, clients, and vendors enhances risk management capacity during crises. Organizations should:

- ➢ Develop contingency plans for regulatory changes.

> Foster long-term relationships with suppliers to ensure flexibility.
> Prioritize employee safety and well-being as a core risk management principle.

Lesson 3: The Power of Agility and Decision-Making in Uncertain Environments

One of the most critical aspects of crisis management is the ability to make swift, well-informed decisions in highly uncertain and rapidly evolving environments. Business leaders and project managers must adapt their strategies on the fly, reallocate resources, and shift priorities in response to real-time challenges. The ability to balance speed and strategic thinking in such situations determines whether a business can survive—or even thrive—during crises.

The Role of Agility in Crisis Management

During a crisis situation, waiting too long to act can exacerbate risks, while rushing into decisions without proper evaluation can lead to costly mistakes. Agility in crisis management is about:

> Quickly identifying key challenges and recalibrating strategies accordingly.
> Balancing risk assessment with decisive action, avoiding decision paralysis.

> Remaining flexible in resource allocation and operational execution.

When the Ebola outbreak created massive disruptions in Liberia, the Conex Petroleum Storage Terminal project faced:

> **Unexpected labor shortages** due to strict travel restrictions and health concerns.
> **Unpredictable regulatory changes** as government agencies imposed new policies.
> **Logistical breakdowns** with delayed shipments of critical materials.

Agility in Action:

> **Workforce Reallocation** – Instead of halting operations, the project team pivoted by training and deploying a local workforce, ensuring steady progress.
> **Dynamic Vendor Sourcing** – Alternative suppliers were identified within the region, bypassing international supply chain delays.
> **Regulatory Adaptation** – The leadership team proactively engaged with authorities, ensuring compliance with new safety measures without stalling work.

Result: Despite severe constraints, the project was completed on time and under budget, saving $2M, thereby reinforcing the value of adaptive decision-making in crisis response.

Key Takeaways: Agility as a Core Competency in Business Development

> ➢ Agility is not just about reacting to crises—it's about proactively adapting and evolving.
> ➢ Quick, informed decision-making is critical during high-risk situations.
> ➢ Leaders must balance immediate problem-solving with long-term strategic vision.
> ➢ Businesses that embrace agility and digital transformation emerge stronger from crises.

By cultivating an agile mindset, business leaders can navigate uncertainty, manage crises effectively, and create new opportunities amid disruption.

Final Thoughts: Turning Crisis into Opportunity

The key takeaway from the two case studies is that crisis management is not just about survival—it's about adaptation, innovation, and long-term growth. Business leaders who embrace agility, leverage technology, and challenge traditional thinking can help their organizations to emerge from crises stronger, more competitive, and better positioned for the future.

In the next section we will explore how First-Principles Thinking can be further applied in crisis management to solve complex business challenges creatively and effectively.

Leveraging First-Principles Thinking for Problem-Solving During Crisis Management

In times of crisis, conventional approaches to problem-solving often fall short. Unprecedented challenges require a fresh perspective—one that goes beyond traditional methods and embraces fundamental truths to generate innovative solutions. This is where first-principles thinking comes into play.

First-principles thinking is a problem-solving approach that involves breaking down complex challenges into their most basic elements and reconstructing solutions from the ground up. Instead of relying on assumptions, industry norms, or best practices, leaders who adopt first-principles thinking strip problems down to their core facts and explore novel ways to solve them.

In business development and crisis management, this methodology helps leaders:

- Overcome constraints by questioning existing processes.
- Develop breakthrough innovations by focusing on fundamental principles.
- Create more efficient, cost-effective, and scalable solutions.

This section explores how first-principles thinking was applied to successfully manage crises in the following two high-stakes scenarios:

> ➢ The $15M Conex Petroleum Storage Terminal Project in Liberia during the Ebola outbreak.
> ➢ The transformation of SAGA's training business during the COVID-19 pandemic.

Case 1: Overcoming Workforce and Operational Challenges During the Ebola Crisis

As described in the previous section, during the Ebola outbreak in West Africa, business activities faced severe disruptions. The Conex Petroleum Storage Terminal Project in Liberia was at risk due to:

> ➢ **Strict movement restrictions** preventing workforce mobility.
> ➢ **Health risks for on-site workers** leading to labor shortages.
> ➢ **Severe delays in the supply chain**, impacting construction timelines.

Conventional Approach: The typical industry response would have been to suspend operations until conditions improved—leading to project delays, financial losses, and reputational damage.

First-Principles Solution: Instead of waiting for the crisis to subside, the project team questioned assumptions about **workforce dependency and supply chain limitations**.

> ➢ **Local Workforce Training:** A decision was made to train and upskill local labor, reducing

reliance on external specialists who couldn't travel due to restrictions.

> **On-Site Health Protocols:** A strict health monitoring system was established, ensuring worker safety while keeping the construction activities up and running.

> **Supply Chain Diversification:** Alternative suppliers within the region were identified to bypass logistical bottlenecks.

Result: The project was completed on schedule, with $2M in cost savings, demonstrating how first-principles thinking enabled a flexible, resource-efficient crisis response.

Case 2: Reinventing Training Through Digital Transformation During COVID-19

The COVID-19 pandemic disrupted SAGA Global's instructor-led training (ILT) business, with travel restrictions and lockdowns rendering in-person training impossible.

Conventional Approach: Many training providers chose to pause operations or wait for restrictions to ease, leading to revenue loss and even loss of clients.

First-Principles Solution: Instead of relying on the traditional ILT model, SAGA's business development team broke down the core elements of training delivery as follows:

- ➢ **What is the fundamental goal of training?** → Knowledge transfer and skill development.
- ➢ **Does it require physical presence?** → Not necessarily; digital platforms can replicate engagement.
- ➢ **What prevents a shift to digital?** → The only constraint is mindset and execution strategy.

By focusing on core principles rather than industry norms, SAGA pivoted to a Virtual Instructor-Led Training (VILT) model that:

- ➢ Eliminated dependency on physical locations.
- ➢ Enhanced engagement through digital tools with analytics for learning enhancement.
- ➢ Expanded the client base by making training accessible across borders.

Result: Not only did the business maintain continuity, but it also became more profitable and scalable, proving that rethinking constraints leads to long-term growth opportunities.

How to Apply First-Principles Thinking in Business Development and Crisis Management

1. Break Down the Problem to Its Core Elements

- ➢ Identify what is absolutely essential versus what is an assumption.
- ➢ Separate industry norms from actual functional requirements.

2. Question Existing Assumptions and Constraints

> - Ask, **"Why is this the way it is?"** instead of accepting conventional wisdom.
> - Challenge traditional solutions by exploring alternative possibilities.

3. Reconstruct a New Solution from the Ground Up

> - Focus on fundamentals and rebuild processes without unnecessary limitations.
> - Apply technology, automation, and creative problem-solving to eliminate inefficiencies.

Final Thoughts: Embracing a Problem-Solving Mindset for Long-Term Success

Crises will always be a part of business, but leaders who embrace first-principles thinking can turn obstacles into opportunities. Whether it is navigating pandemic like situation, economic downturns, or geopolitical disruptions, businesses that question assumptions, focus on fundamentals, and innovate solutions from scratch will emerge stronger.

By applying first-principles thinking to crisis management and business development, companies can:

> - Future-proof their operations against uncertainty.

> Develop innovative, scalable solutions that go beyond short-term fixes.
> Outperform competitors who rely on conventional approaches.

This chapter has demonstrated how bold problem-solving, technological adaptability, and strategic agility create business resilience and long-term success. As industries continue evolving, organizations must develop a mindset that not only responds to crises but leverages them as catalysts for innovation and expansion.

Chapter 8: Understanding the Role of Change Management in Business Development

In today's fast-evolving business landscape, adaptability is not just an asset—it is a necessity. Change is no longer an occasional event but an ongoing process that organizations must embrace to remain competitive. Markets shift, consumer behaviors, regulations change, and technological advancements redefine industries. Business development, being at the forefront of organizational growth, must be aligned with effective change management strategies to ensure long-term success.

However, change—despite its necessity—is often met with resistance. Whether it involves a new market entry, restructuring operations, implementing new technologies, or evolving a company's strategic vision, organizations must navigate change with a structured, well-executed approach. When managed effectively, change leads to enhanced efficiency, innovation, and market leadership. When mishandled, it can result in organizational disruption, employee disengagement, and business stagnation.

This chapter delves into the critical role of change management in business development, exploring why change is essential for growth, best practices for leading organizational transformation, and a real-world case study on restructuring at Khartoum Refinery Corporation, where strategic change was implemented amid complex political and economic challenges.

Why Change Management is essential for a Business

Change is the driving force behind business expansion, market adaptation, and long-term sustainability. Companies that fail to evolve, risk falling behind in an increasingly competitive environment. The ability to manage change effectively determines whether an organization thrives or struggles.

Change Management is essential for an Organization's Growth and Competitive Advantage due to the following reasons:

1. **Adapting to Market Shifts** – Industries are constantly evolving due to consumer behavior changes, regulatory updates, and technological disruptions. Businesses that anticipate and adapt to these shifts can gain a first-mover advantage and capitalize on emerging opportunities.
2. **Enhancing Operational Efficiency** – Change management often involves process optimization, automation, and structural improvements that lead to cost reduction and increased productivity.
3. **Staying Ahead of Competitors** – The ability to adapt quickly in response to market dynamics gives companies a strategic edge. Organizations that resist change often struggle to keep up with innovative competitors who leverage transformation for growth.
4. **Driving Innovation and Scalability** – Companies that embrace change create a culture

of continuous improvement, fostering innovation and enabling them to scale operations effectively.

5. **Aligning with Long-Term Strategic Goals** – Change initiatives help organizations stay aligned with their vision and mission, ensuring that every transformation effort contributes to sustainable business development.

⇒ **The Impact of Change on Business Strategy and Market Positioning**

Business strategy is not static—it evolves based on industry trends, internal capabilities, and external disruptions. Effective change management ensures that strategic shifts are smooth, structured, and goal-oriented. Key areas where change influences business strategy include:

➢ **Expansion into New Markets** – Entering new territories requires modifications in operational structure, compliance strategies, and marketing approaches.

➢ **Mergers, Acquisitions, and Restructuring** – These transitions reshape organizational hierarchy, corporate culture, and market presence, necessitating careful change management to prevent resistance and inefficiencies.

➢ **Technology Integration** – The adoption of AI, automation, and digital solutions transforms business operations but requires well-planned change implementation strategies to ensure successful adoption.

➢ **Crisis Response and Recovery** – Unexpected economic downturns, global pandemics, and geopolitical uncertainties demand quick yet structured change strategies to keep businesses resilient.

With change being a constant factor in business development, organizations must implement proven frameworks to manage transitions effectively and minimize disruptions. The next section explores best practices and key methodologies for leading effective change management in line with the Organizational goals.

⇒ **Aligning Change Initiatives with Business Development Goals**

For change to be successful in a business development context, it must be purposeful, structured, and directly linked to the broader growth strategy of the organization. Without this alignment, change efforts may lead to internal confusion, operational inefficiencies, and resistance from key stakeholders. Business development professionals play a critical role in ensuring that any transformation—whether structural, strategic, or technological—drives tangible business outcomes while maintaining continuity and stakeholder confidence.

Here are the key principles for ensuring that change initiatives are aligned with business development goals:

1. Strategic Alignment: Connecting Change with Business Growth and Long-Term Vision

Change should never be pursued for the sake of change— it must have a clear business rationale. Organizations that successfully implement change ensure that every initiative is:

> **Aligned with the company's mission and vision** – Business growth depends on a strong sense of purpose. Change should reinforce the long-term objectives of the company, whether it is expanding into new markets, enhancing operational efficiency, or improving customer satisfaction.
> **Linked to key performance indicators (KPIs)** – Establishing measurable goals ensures that change efforts have a quantifiable impact on business development, whether through revenue growth, cost savings, increased market share, or enhanced customer engagement.
> **Implemented in phases to ensure scalability** – Business development professionals must consider the timing, scope, and scalability of change initiatives to prevent operational disruptions while ensuring a smooth transition.

Example: A company expanding into an international market must align its change strategy with local regulatory requirements, consumer behavior insights, and operational feasibility to ensure a successful market entry.

2. Stakeholder Engagement: Keeping Clients, Employees, and Investors Informed and Involved

One of the biggest reasons why change initiatives fail is due to a lack of buy-in from key stakeholders. Employees, customers, and investors need to understand the purpose and benefits of the transformation in order to support it.

- ➢ **Employee Buy-In & Engagement** – Employees who feel disconnected from the change process are more likely to resist it. Transparent communication, training, and involvement in decision-making can significantly improve change adoption rates.
- ➢ **Client & Customer Alignment** – When changes affect service offerings, product availability, or business relationships, clients must be kept informed and reassured about how the transformation benefits them.
- ➢ **Investor Confidence** – Investors seek stability and long-term value creation. Any change initiative should be articulated in a way that demonstrates financial sustainability, competitive positioning, and risk mitigation strategies.

Example: A global consulting firm shifting to a digital-first service delivery model must ensure that clients are educated and prepared for the transition, ensuring continued engagement and satisfaction.

3. Data-Driven Decision-Making: Refining Change Strategies with Analytics

In an era where data is at the core of business decision-making, successful change initiatives rely on real-time insights, predictive analytics, and performance tracking to ensure their effectiveness.

- ➢ **Using Market Data to Shape Change Strategies** – Business development teams should use competitive intelligence, customer insights, and industry forecasts to inform their change management approach.

- ➢ **Monitoring Change Adoption in Real Time** – Organizations can leverage AI-driven analytics and feedback mechanisms to measure how employees, clients, and stakeholders are responding to change efforts.
- ➢ **Adapting Strategies Based on Measurable Results** – If a change initiative is not delivering the desired impact, organizations must pivot quickly, refine their approach, and implement corrective measures.

Example: A multinational company transitioning from manual supply chain management to AI-powered logistics must continuously monitor inventory turnover rates, order accuracy, and fulfillment speed to evaluate the success of the transformation.

To understand how these best practices play out in real-world scenarios, the next section examines a case study where I led the organizational restructuring and change management initiative at Khartoum Refinery Corporation, Sudan, where strategic change was implemented amid political and economic challenges.

Case Study: Organizational Restructuring at Khartoum Refinery Corporation

Organizational restructuring is one of the most challenging and high-stakes transformations a company can undergo. The Khartoum Refinery Corporation (KRC), a major refining facility in Sudan, faced significant challenges that necessitated a comprehensive restructuring initiative to achieve operational excellence. This case study examines how strategic change was implemented in a politically and economically unstable environment, the key challenges encountered, and the lessons learned from the experience.

⇒ The Challenge: Implementing Change Amid Political and Economic Instability

The KRC restructuring initiative was driven by the need to enhance operational efficiency, optimize workforce structures, and implement global best practices. However, the process faced multiple political, economic, and organizational barriers, including:

1. **Political and Regulatory Uncertainty**

   - Sudan faced ongoing political instability, including a military coup in October 2021, which disrupted governmental functions and slowed decision-making processes.
   - Changing government regulations and economic policies made long-term planning difficult, requiring a flexible and adaptive restructuring approach.

2. **Resistance to Change from Leadership and Employees**

   - Management and staff unions were resistant to restructuring, fearing job losses, uncertainty, and changes to the traditional corporate structure.
   - Employees had low confidence in the success of the restructuring process, leading to internal resistance and slow adoption of new processes.

3. **Inefficiencies in Organizational Structure and Decision-Making**

> ➢ Outdated decision-making processes and bureaucratic inefficiencies led to delays in implementing critical operational improvements.
> ➢ Lack of performance accountability resulted in inefficiencies in refinery operations, increasing costs and reducing productivity.

4. **Economic Pressures and Financial Constraints**

> ➢ The volatile economic environment in Sudan made funding for restructuring initiatives difficult.
> ➢ Budget constraints required cost-effective restructuring solutions that balanced financial feasibility with long-term operational improvements.

⇒ **The Change Management Strategy**

To overcome these challenges, a structured and strategic approach was adopted, leveraging global best practices in organizational restructuring while ensuring alignment with KRC's operational goals and the local economic context. The restructuring exercise was guided by four core principles:

1. **Benchmarking Global Best Practices in Refinery Operations**

> ➢ SAGA SMEs (Subject Matter Experts) conducted an organizational benchmarking study, comparing KRC's structure with that of

internationally benchmarked Petroleum refineries to identify gaps in efficiency, leadership, and performance metrics.
- SAGA team established a revised organizational hierarchy that optimized decision-making channels, reduced bureaucracy, and improved efficiency.
- It was recommended to adopt automation and digital tools to streamline workflow and enhance operational transparency.

2. Stakeholder Engagement and Strategic Communication

- A structured communication plan was implemented to engage with leadership, employees, and external regulatory bodies, ensuring alignment on restructuring objectives.
- SAGA team conducted series of meetings, workshops, and training sessions to educate employees on the restructuring benefits and alleviate concerns about job security.
- I continued my engagement with KRC Management to build trust through transparency, providing employees with clear career progression pathways and reassurance that the restructuring aimed at long-term organizational sustainability rather than immediate cost-cutting.

3. Workforce Optimization and Performance Enhancement

- Implemented a talent optimization strategy, ensuring that each employee's role was

> aligned with organizational objectives and eliminating redundant positions while focusing on upskilling and redeployment.
> Introduced a performance-based incentive system, ensuring that employees and leadership were rewarded for efficiency improvements and adherence to restructuring goals.
> Launched leadership training programs to equip mid- and senior-level managers with the skills necessary to drive organizational change effectively.

The Outcome: A Successful Implementation of Organizational Restructuring Initiative at KRC

Despite the challenging environment, the restructuring initiative led to tangible improvements in KRC's operations as follows:

> Achieved 90% acceptance of the proposed restructuring plan, demonstrating successful stakeholder engagement.
> Operational efficiency improved by 22%, due to optimized workflows and enhanced decision-making processes.
> Cost savings of $1.3M annually were realized by streamlining workforce structures and adopting lean operational methodologies.
> It positioned KRC to achieve global benchmarks in operational excellence, making the refinery more competitive in the international market.

Lessons Learned: Key Takeaways from the KRC Restructuring Initiative

The success of the restructuring initiative at KRC provides valuable lessons for business leaders and organizations looking to implement large-scale change management programs:

1. Strong Leadership Buy-In is Critical

> ➢ Without commitment from top leadership, change initiatives face internal resistance and risk failure. Gaining executive-level support ensures that restructuring objectives are successfully implemented.

2. Stakeholder Engagement and Transparent Communication Reduce Resistance

> ➢ Employees, management, and external stakeholders must be actively engaged and reassured throughout the process. Transparent dialogue, structured training, and clear incentives help reduce resistance to change.

3. A Phased Approach to Change Minimizes Disruptions

> ➢ Instead of implementing drastic restructuring all at once, a gradual, step-by-step approach allows organizations to identify potential roadblocks early and adjust strategies accordingly.

4. Economic and Political Realities must be Factored into Planning

> ➢ Organizations operating in unstable environments must remain flexible and agile,

ensuring that restructuring efforts are sustainable even amid political and economic uncertainties.

5. Workforce Optimization is more Effective than Layoffs

> ➢ Instead of mass job cuts, a strategy that prioritizes redeployment, reskilling, and realignment ensures long-term workforce sustainability without eroding employee morale.

Final Thoughts: The Power of Change Management in Business Development

The restructuring exercise at Khartoum Refinery Corporation, Sudan demonstrated the critical role of effective change management in business development. Despite political instability, financial constraints, and internal resistance, a well-structured approach focused on best practices, stakeholder engagement, and workforce optimization ensured that the refinery was transformed into a more efficient, globally competitive entity.

For business development leaders, the key takeaway is clear: embracing change, fostering a culture of adaptability, and aligning restructuring efforts with long-term business objectives can turn even the most challenging transformations into opportunities for growth and excellence.

Chapter 9: Strategic Alliances in International Business Development

In today's globalized economy, businesses no longer operate in isolation. In fact, in today's business world, success is often defined by an organization's ability to build strategic alliances. Whether through joint ventures, partnerships, or long-term collaborations, companies that form strong alliances gain access to new markets, resources, expertise, and competitive advantages that would otherwise be difficult to achieve independently. International business development today thrives on collaboration, and strategic alliances are the cornerstone of sustainable global expansion.

However, forging successful alliances is not without its challenges. Cultural differences, regulatory complexities, geopolitical risks, and operational hurdles can complicate even the most promising partnerships. Navigating these complexities requires a deep understanding of regional business practices, government policies, and market-specific challenges. When executed well, strategic alliances unlock unparalleled growth opportunities, as demonstrated by the case of establishing a partnership with Arcelor Mittal Liberia, which successfully addressed cost overruns and revived critical infrastructure projects.

Case Study: Establishing Strategic Alliance with Arcelor Mittal Liberia

In the realm of international business development, collaborations with established industry leaders can drive significant growth and create long-term value. One such strategic alliance was formed between my organization i.e. SAGA Global Consultants and Arcelor Mittal Liberia, aimed at overcoming cost overruns and operational inefficiencies in the storage and distribution infrastructure of Arcelor Mittal in Liberia.

The alliance was not merely a business partnership—it was a high-stakes collaboration in a challenging economic and regulatory environment. The project had been stalled for over eight years due to financial constraints and inefficiencies in resource management. The challenge was not just in executing the project but in reviving stakeholder confidence, ensuring financial feasibility, and navigating complex regulatory landscapes.

⇒ **The Challenge: Addressing Cost Overruns and Operational Stagnation**

Arcelor Mittal Liberia, a major player in West Africa's mining and steel industry, had embarked on an infrastructure expansion project involving the rehabilitation of storage and distribution facilities at two key sites in Liberia; viz. at Buchanan and Tokadeh. However, the project faced significant hurdles as follows:

1. **Cost Overruns and Financial Inefficiencies**

- ➢ The project was interrupted during the Ebola outbreak in the region in 2014-15.
- ➢ Over the years, the project had suffered from budget misalignment, inefficient resource allocation, and escalating costs, making further investment questionable.
- ➢ Financial justification was required to secure board-level approval for project continuation.

2. **Regulatory and Compliance Challenges**

- ➢ Liberia's evolving industrial and environmental regulations added complexity to the project.
- ➢ Aligning stakeholder expectations with government requirements was crucial to ensure approvals and compliance.

3. **Underutilization of Existing Materials and Delayed Execution**

- ➢ A significant amount of on-site construction materials had remained unused for years, requiring an assessment of what could be salvaged and optimized.
- ➢ Delays had led to depreciation of critical assets, increasing the need for cost-effective solutions.

⇒ **The Approach: Structuring a Strategic Alliance for Mutual Success**

Understanding the complexity of the situation, our team at SAGA adopted a systematic approach with a comprehensive methodology as follows:

1. Conducting a Comprehensive Cost Analysis and Feasibility Assessment

> ➢ A deep-dive financial review was conducted to identify inefficiencies in the original project execution plan.
> ➢ A cost-optimization framework was developed, ensuring that project investments delivered maximum value with minimal waste.
> ➢ The assessment prioritized the reallocation of existing materials, reducing the need for additional procurement.

Impact: The revised cost structure resulted in a 13% reduction in estimated project costs, amounting to savings of $5.78M, making the project financially viable.

2. Aligning with Government and Regulatory Authorities

> ➢ SAGA advised Arcelor Mittal Liberia team to engage Liberian regulatory bodies early in the process to ensure that the revised project plan complied with local industrial policies and environmental laws.
> ➢ A transparent documentation and reporting system was established, ensuring all compliance requirements were met proactively.

Impact: Government stakeholders approved the revised strategy, allowing for an accelerated project restart with minimal regulatory friction.

3. Strengthening Stakeholder Collaboration and Communication

> ➢ A joint task force was created between SAGA and Arcelor Mittal Liberia to ensure seamless execution.
> ➢ Regular stakeholder engagement meetings were conducted, reinforcing confidence and buy-in from investors, local authorities, and suppliers.

Impact: The strengthened partnership re-established trust, securing final board approval for the project's continuation.

⇒ **The Outcome: A Successful Revival of a Stalled Project**

Through strategic restructuring, financial optimization, and stakeholder engagement, the strategic alliance helped to achieve the following outcome:

> ➢ Total project costs were reduced by 13% ($5.78M savings), making the project financially feasible.
> ➢ Government and regulatory approvals were proactively secured, ensuring full compliance with local laws.
> ➢ Restored confidence with the Investors and stakeholders thereby enabling further capital allocation.
> ➢ Both the teams jointly established a streamlined execution framework, reducing operational inefficiencies.

This strategic alliance not only revitalized a struggling project but also strengthened long-term collaboration between SAGA Global Consultants and Arcelor Mittal Liberia, positioning both companies for future joint ventures and regional expansion.

⇒ **Lessons Learned: Best Practices for Building Strategic Alliances**

This case study highlights the following key takeaways for companies looking to establish successful international business alliances:

1. Early Cost and Feasibility Assessments Ensure Financial Viability

> ➢ Conducting cost-benefit analyses allows for structured negotiations and improved financial planning.

2. Regulatory and Stakeholder Alignment Is Critical

> ➢ Engaging government bodies and investors early in the process minimizes legal hurdles and accelerates project execution.

3. Clear Roles and Risk Distribution Strengthen Alliances

> ➢ Defining clear deliverables, shared risks, and incentives prevents conflicts and ensures mutual accountability.

4. Long-Term Partnership Thinking Leads to Sustainable Growth

> Strategic alliances should be structured beyond a single project, fostering opportunities for continuous collaboration and market expansion.

Final Thoughts: The Role of Strategic Alliances in Business Development

In international business development, collaborations are no longer optional—they are imperative for sustainable growth. Strategic alliances unlock market opportunities, enhance operational capabilities, and mitigate risks associated with entering new territories.

The success of our partnership with Arcelor Mittal Liberia demonstrates how effective alliances are built on financial prudence, stakeholder alignment, and shared-value creation. As companies continue to expand globally, business leaders must develop the skills to forge, sustain, and optimize partnerships that drive long-term success.

The next section will delve into navigating cultural and regulatory complexities in global business partnerships, ensuring that strategic alliances are structured to withstand regional and operational challenges.

Insights on Navigating Cultural and Regulatory Complexities in International Business Alliances

Expanding into international markets offers immense growth opportunities, but it also introduces a set of challenges that businesses must navigate skillfully. One of the most critical aspects of forming successful strategic alliances in global business development is understanding and adapting to cultural and regulatory complexities. These factors can significantly influence decision-making, operational execution, contract negotiations, and long-term collaboration success.

Businesses that fail to address cultural differences and regulatory hurdles often struggle with misalignment, delays, compliance issues, and breakdowns in partnerships. On the other hand, companies that embrace cultural intelligence, regulatory expertise, and adaptable business strategies gain a competitive edge in global expansion. This section explores the key cultural and regulatory challenges businesses face and how to effectively navigate them when forming strategic alliances.

The Role of Cultural Intelligence in International Business Alliances

Culture plays a fundamental role in shaping business etiquette, negotiation styles, decision-making processes, and corporate structures. Ignoring cultural nuances can lead to miscommunication, mistrust, and failed partnerships.

⇒ **Key Cultural Challenges in International Alliances**

1. Different Negotiation Styles and Business Etiquette

> In Western markets, negotiations are often direct, data-driven, and result-oriented.

> In Asian, Middle Eastern, and African markets, negotiations tend to be relationship-driven, hierarchical, and patience-intensive.
> Failing to adapt to these cultural preferences can derail negotiations and strain business relationships.

2. Decision-Making Processes and Corporate Hierarchy

> Some cultures prioritize fast decision-making and autonomy, while others rely on group consensus and hierarchical approval structures.
> In markets like Japan, the Middle East, and West Africa, corporate decisions often require multiple levels of approval, making processes more structured but slower.
> Business leaders must be patient and adaptable, ensuring that they align with local decision-making norms.

3. Communication Barriers and Language Differences

> Misinterpretation of emails, contracts, or verbal discussions can lead to misunderstandings in international partnerships.
> Cultural sensitivity around tone, body language, and indirect communication is essential.
> Using local business liaisons, translators, and culturally aware team members can bridge the communication gap effectively.

⇒ **Strategies to Navigate Cultural Complexities**

1. Develop Cultural Intelligence (CQ)

> Train business development teams in cross-cultural negotiation and relationship management.
> Invest in local business consultants or cultural advisors to ensure smooth communication.

2. Adapt Negotiation Styles to Match Cultural Expectations

> **In high-context cultures (Middle East, Africa, Asia)** → Build trust before discussing business terms.
> **In low-context cultures (U.S., Germany, Netherlands)** → Focus on efficiency, clarity, and direct engagement.

3. Establish Relationship-Based Business Development Approaches

> Many emerging markets prioritize long-term trust over short-term profits.
> Frequent in-person meetings, hospitality gestures, and long-term commitment discussions enhance credibility.

4. Leverage Local Market Experts and Advisors

> It is advisable to appoint local representatives or consultants who understand business etiquette, regulatory requirements, and economic conditions.

⇒ **Navigating Regulatory Challenges in International Business Alliances**

Beyond cultural differences, regulatory frameworks differ widely across international markets, affecting business entry, contracts, taxation, employment laws, and operational execution. Ignoring or misinterpreting these regulations can lead to delays, financial penalties, or legal disputes.

Common Regulatory Challenges in Global Business Expansion are as follows:

1. Governmental Policies and Foreign Investment Restrictions

- ➢ Some countries impose strict limitations on foreign ownership and require joint ventures with local companies.
- ➢ For example: In the Middle East and parts of Africa, foreign businesses must often partner with local entities to gain market access.

2. Taxation and Trade Compliance

- ➢ Differences in corporate tax structures, tariffs, and import/export duties can impact profitability.
- ➢ For example: Some countries provide tax incentives for foreign investors, while others impose high tariffs on imported goods to protect domestic industries.

3. Employment Laws and Labor Compliance

> Workforce regulations vary, including hiring restrictions, labor contracts, and employee benefits requirements.
> For example: The European Union enforces strict labor protection laws, while some Asian markets allow for more flexible workforce regulations.

4. Contract Enforcement and Dispute Resolution Mechanisms

> Some legal systems favor local businesses in contractual disputes, making clear legal frameworks essential for risk mitigation.
> Arbitration mechanisms like the International Chamber of Commerce (ICC) or local legal arbitration courts must be considered when structuring agreements.

⇒ **Strategies to Overcome Regulatory Hurdles**

1. Engage Local Legal Experts and Compliance Advisors

> Partner with local legal firms or consultants who specialize in foreign business regulations.
> Ensure contractual agreements align with local laws and international arbitration mechanisms.

2. Structure Business Models to Comply with Local Laws

➤ In countries with restrictions on foreign ownership, form joint ventures or strategic partnerships with trusted local firms.
➤ Adapt corporate structures (e.g., licensing agreements, franchising models) to ensure regulatory compliance while maintaining business control.

3. Monitor Regulatory Changes Proactively

➤ Governments frequently update foreign business policies, requiring companies to stay informed on evolving laws.
➤ Establish a regulatory affairs team or advisory board to track compliance updates.

4. Implement Strong Governance and Compliance Mechanisms

➤ Ensure all business activities adhere to ethical standards and anti-corruption policies to maintain regulatory approval and business credibility.

Adapting to Regional Challenges in International Markets

Each region presents unique economic, political, and business challenges that require tailored strategies. Businesses must develop market-specific approaches rather than applying one-size-fits-all strategies.

⇒ **Key Regional Challenges and Adaptation Strategies**

1. Doing Business in Emerging Markets (Africa, Latin America, Southeast Asia)

Challenges:

- Political instability and regulatory unpredictability.
- Underdeveloped infrastructure affecting logistics and supply chain efficiency.
- Higher risks of corruption and bureaucratic hurdles.

Adaptation Strategies:

- Build long-term local partnerships to gain government and industry credibility.
- Invest in risk assessment models and geopolitical analysis tools.
- Establish localized operational hubs to manage supply chain disruptions.

2. Expanding into Highly Regulated Economies (Europe, Middle East, China)

Challenges:

- Complex compliance and data protection laws (e.g., GDPR in Europe).
- State-controlled industries with strict regulations on foreign entities.

Adaptation Strategies:

- Leverage local legal expertise and compliance teams to ensure full regulatory adherence.

> Consider regional partnerships or licensing models to navigate restrictive laws.
> Invest in corporate social responsibility (CSR) initiatives to align with local policies.

Final Thoughts: Mastering Cultural and Regulatory Navigation for International Success

Thus, strategic alliances in international business development require a deep understanding of cultural sensitivities and regulatory frameworks. Companies that invest in cultural intelligence, proactive regulatory compliance, and tailored regional strategies will gain a sustainable advantage in global markets.

The next section will explore practical strategies for structuring successful international partnerships, ensuring that alliances are built for long-term value creation and operational resilience.

Structuring Strategic Alliances for Long-Term Business Growth

Establishing a strategic alliance is not just about securing a one-time business deal—it is about building long-term, mutually beneficial partnerships that foster sustainable business growth. Successful alliances go beyond transactional agreements; they involve shared vision, aligned goals, and well-defined frameworks for execution and governance.

For international business development, structuring an alliance requires careful planning, due diligence, and a clear strategy for collaboration. A poorly structured partnership can lead to operational inefficiencies, financial losses, and reputational damage, while a well-structured alliance can unlock new markets, drive innovation, and create long-term competitive advantages.

This section outlines the key elements required to structure a successful strategic alliance, including defining objectives, risk-sharing mechanisms, governance models, and performance evaluation metrics.

⇒ **Defining the Objectives and Scope of the Alliance**

The foundation of any strategic alliance lies in a clear definition of its purpose, expected outcomes, and long-term vision. Without a well-defined scope, there is a chance of misalignment between partners that can lead to conflicts, operational inefficiencies, and missed opportunities.

Key Considerations while defining Alliance Objectives

1. Strategic Fit:

> ➤ How does the alliance align with the business development goals of both parties?
> ➤ What market gaps or opportunities does this partnership aim to address?

2. Value Creation for Both Partners:

> ➤ How will each partner benefit financially, operationally, and strategically from the alliance?

> What core competencies and resources do each party bring to the table?

3. Geographical and Industry Scope:

> Will the alliance be regional, global, or industry-specific?
> What are the primary and secondary business activities covered under the partnership?

4. Timeframe and Evolution Plan:

> Is the alliance short-term (project-based) or long-term (continuous partnership)?
> How will the alliance evolve with market trends, regulatory changes, and industry innovations?

⇒ **Structuring a Risk-Sharing and Governance Model**

Every alliance involves a degree of risk, whether it is financial, operational, legal, or market-related. A successful strategic alliance must have a risk-sharing framework that ensures both parties contribute fairly while mitigating potential losses and liabilities.

Risk-Sharing Models in Strategic Alliances

1. Joint Investment Models:

> Structuring financial contributions proportionally based on expertise, market access, or operational responsibilities.

➢ Defining mechanisms for profit-sharing, cost distribution, and reinvestment in future projects.

2. Legal and Compliance Risk Management:

➢ Ensuring that contracts are aligned with international regulatory standards and protect both parties' interests.
➢ Defining liability clauses and dispute resolution mechanisms in case of contractual disagreements.

3. Market and Operational Risk Allocation:

- Assigning market expansion responsibilities based on regional expertise (e.g., one partner handles regulatory approvals while the other focuses on sales and distribution).
- Creating contingency plans for economic downturns, political instability, or changes in trade policies.

⇒ Establishing Clear Governance and Decision-Making Structures

Governance is the backbone of a successful strategic alliance. Without a structured governance model, alliances can descend into conflicts, inefficiencies, and power struggles.

Key Governance Structures for Strategic Alliances

1. Joint Steering Committees & Leadership Roles:

> Establishing a leadership board with representatives from both organizations to oversee strategy and execution.
> Defining decision-making authority and escalation protocols to resolve disputes efficiently.

2. Operational Guidelines and Performance Monitoring:

> Creating a standardized operating model that defines how teams collaborate, report progress, and manage project execution.
> Implementing data-driven performance tracking to measure key metrics such as revenue growth, cost savings, and market penetration.

3. Conflict Resolution Mechanisms:

- Pre-determining mediation and arbitration processes in case of disagreements.
- Including exit strategies and dissolution terms in the event that one party chooses to leave the alliance.

⇒ **Measuring the Success of the Alliance**

A well-structured strategic alliance must include quantifiable performance metrics that track the success and impact of the partnership. These metrics help in evaluating ROI, identifying areas for improvement, and ensuring the longevity of the collaboration.

Key Performance Indicators (KPIs) for Strategic Alliances

1. Financial Performance:

> Revenue growth, cost savings, and profitability improvements resulting from the alliance.
> Actual Return on investment (ROI) compared to initial projections.

2. Market Impact & Expansion:

> Market share growth and penetration in new regions.
> Volume of new business generated through the partnership.

3. Operational Efficiency Gains:

> Reduction in project execution timelines and budget overruns.
> Improvements in supply chain efficiency, productivity, and quality control.

4. Stakeholder Satisfaction and Continuity:

> Strength of relationships with clients, regulators, and investors due to the alliance.
> Likelihood of extending the partnership to future projects.

Final Thoughts: Building Alliances That Drive Long-Term Growth

Strategic alliances, when structured correctly, can become powerful engines for business expansion, risk mitigation, and market penetration. Companies that invest in clear governance, well-defined risk-sharing mechanisms, and measurable success metrics will maximize the value of their partnerships and position themselves for long-term industry leadership.

The key takeaways for structuring sustainable strategic alliances are:

> - Define clear objectives and align them with long-term business growth strategies.
> - Develop a balanced risk-sharing framework to ensure financial and operational stability.
> - Establish governance structures that enable collaborative decision-making.
> - Continuously measure performance and adapt strategies to ensure ongoing success.

As businesses continue to expand into new international markets, strategic partnerships will become even more critical for driving innovation, operational efficiency, and competitive advantage. Companies that master the art of structuring alliances effectively will not only enhance their global footprint but also create long-term business value that withstands economic and market fluctuations.

Chapter 10: Reflections and Takeaways

Business development is not just a function—it is a journey of continuous learning, adaptation, and strategic foresight. Over the years, industries have evolved, markets have transformed, and technological advancements have reshaped the way businesses operate. Yet, the fundamental principles of business growth, relationship management, and strategic execution remain unchanged. Success in business development is not solely about securing deals; it is about creating value, building sustainable partnerships, and having the agility to navigate an ever-changing global landscape.

As this book comes to a close, it is essential to pause and reflect on the key lessons, challenges, and successes that have shaped my journey. From negotiating high-stakes contracts to leading business expansions in complex international markets, every experience has contributed to a deeper understanding of what it takes to build, sustain, and grow businesses across industries and geographies. This chapter will summarize the most valuable insights gained from over two decades of my work experience in the Energy sector with specialization in International Business Development. These insights would offer guidance to aspiring professionals, and explore the evolving future of business development, particularly in the energy sector and beyond.

Key Lessons Learned from Over Two Decades in the Industry

Over the past twenty years, I have had the privilege of working across multiple industries, geographies, and business landscapes, witnessing firsthand the challenges, triumphs, and transformations that define business development. From complex negotiations in international markets to navigating economic downturns, geopolitical shifts, and technological revolutions, every experience has reinforced key principles that are fundamental to successful ventures.

The following are the most valuable lessons I have learned, shaped by real-world experiences in business expansion, strategic partnerships, crisis management, and market growth.

1. Business Development is a Strategic Function, Not Just Sales

One of the biggest misconceptions about business development is that it is just about selling services or acquiring clients. In reality, business development is a strategic function that goes far beyond sales. It involves:

- **Market Research & Opportunity Analysis** – Understanding where opportunities exist and how to position your business for long-term growth.
- **Stakeholder Engagement & Relationship Building** – Forming meaningful partnerships that create sustainable business value.

- ➢ **Problem-Solving & Value Creation** – Developing solutions tailored to client needs, rather than just pitching a service or product.
- ➢ **Long-Term Vision & Execution** – Business growth requires a roadmap, patience, and a strategic approach to scaling operations successfully.

Lesson#1: *Successful business development professionals are not just dealmakers—they are market strategists, problem solvers, and visionaries.*

2. Relationships are the True Currency of Business

While revenue and profitability are key indicators of success, the foundation of long-term business growth is built on strong relationships. Deals may be won through strategy, but they are sustained through trust and reliability.

- ➢ **Partnerships Matter More Than Transactions** – A single deal can bring in revenue, but a strong partnership can create a pipeline of recurring business opportunities.
- ➢ **Trust Takes Years to Build and Seconds to Lose** – Always honor commitments, deliver on promises, and prioritize integrity.
- ➢ **Listening is More Powerful Than Selling** – Understanding client pain points and strategic needs leads to better solutions and stronger partnerships.

Lesson#2: *Business development is fundamentally about relationships. A well-nurtured professional network can unlock more opportunities than any sales pitch ever could.*

3. Adaptability is the Key to Thriving in a Changing World

Markets evolve. Industries transform. Technologies disrupt. The only businesses and professionals that survive are the ones that adapt.

> ➤ **Be Willing to Adapt** – Companies that fail to adjust to market trends eventually become obsolete. Business development professionals must always stay ahead of industry shifts.
> ➤ **Embrace Digital Transformation** – AI, automation, and data-driven insights are reshaping business strategy. The ability to leverage technology creates a significant competitive advantage.
> ➤ **Learn Continuously** – Staying relevant in business requires a commitment to lifelong learning, industry insights, and skill development.

Lesson#3: *The ability to adapt and evolve is more valuable than any single skill set. Change is not an obstacle—it is an opportunity.*

4. Crisis Creates Opportunity

Some of the greatest business transformations occur during periods of crisis. Economic downturns, geopolitical instability, or global disruptions can create market uncertainty—but also present new opportunities.

> **Crisis Forces Innovation** – Many of the most successful business strategies were born out of necessity during uncertain times.
> **Companies That Adapt During Crisis Emerge Stronger** – Businesses that adapt strategically during downturns often gain a competitive edge over those that remain stagnant.
> **Risk Management is Non-Negotiable** – Effective crisis management and contingency planning ensure long-term resilience.

Lesson#4: *Every crisis presents a choice: resist and struggle, or adapt and thrive. Business leaders who see challenges as opportunities create lasting success.*

5. Success in International Business Requires Cultural Intelligence

Expanding into global markets is not just about understanding economic trends—it's about navigating cultural, legal, and regulatory landscapes.

> **Every Market Has Unique Business Norms** – A strategy that works in Europe may not work in Asia, the Middle East, or Africa.
> **Understanding Cultural Sensitivities Leads to Better Negotiations** – Business is not just about logic; it's about relationships, etiquette, and trust-building across cultures.

> **Local Partnerships Are Essential for Market Entry** – Working with local stakeholders, advisors, and regulators smoothens international expansion.

Lesson#5: *Cultural awareness is a competitive advantage in global business. The best business development professionals respect, learn from, and adapt to diverse market environments.*

6. Business Development is a Marathon, not a Sprint

Success in business development does not happen overnight. It takes persistence, patience, and long-term strategic execution.

> **Reputation is Built Over Time** – Every deal, every interaction, every decision contributes to a company's reputation in the industry.
> **Trust is Earned, Not Assumed** – Consistently delivering value builds credibility that lasts for decades.
> **Short-Term Gains Should Never Compromise Long-Term Strategy** – Prioritizing quick wins over sustainable growth is a mistake that many businesses regret later.

Lesson#6: *The most successful business leaders play the long game. They focus on sustainable growth, strategic partnerships, and legacy-building—not just short-term profits.*

Advice for Aspiring Business Development Professionals

Business development is one of the most dynamic, and rewarding fields in the corporate world. It requires a combination of strategic foresight, relationship-building, negotiation expertise, and problem-solving skills. For those who are new to the field or looking to accelerate their career in business development, understanding the fundamentals, best practices, and industry nuances is crucial to long-term success.

Unlike traditional sales roles, business development professionals must think beyond closing deals—they must identify market opportunities, establish long-term partnerships, drive strategic initiatives, and align business objectives with industry trends. With global markets evolving rapidly and technological advancements transforming the business dynamics, the next generation of business development leaders must be adaptable, forward-thinking, and innovative.

Below are five critical pieces of advice that every aspiring business development professional should embrace to build a successful and sustainable career in this ever-evolving field.

1. Master the Art of Long-Term Thinking

One of the most significant differences between average and great business development professionals is their perspective on growth. Many professionals focus solely on short-term deals, quick wins, and immediate revenue generation. However, the most impactful business development leaders think long-term, prioritizing sustainable relationships and strategic market positioning over short-term gains. Their strategies are governed by the following core philosophies:

> **Build for the Future:** The deals you close today should pave the way for larger opportunities tomorrow.

> **Prioritize Trust Over Transactions:** A single contract may last a few years, but a strong relationship with a key client or partner can last a lifetime.

> **Develop a Visionary Mindset:** Instead of just thinking about the next deal, think about how you can shape industry trends, expand in different geographies, and position your organization as a market leader.

For Example: Companies that invested in digital transformation and AI-powered business development strategies before the COVID-19 pandemic were better positioned to adapt and thrive compared to those that resisted change.

2. Embrace Lifelong Learning and Industry Awareness

The business development landscape is constantly evolving, driven by new market trends, regulatory changes, and technological innovations. Professionals who stay informed and continuously upgrade their knowledge will always remain ahead of the curve.

To effectively navigate this dynamic environment, business development professionals must:

- ➢ **Stay Updated on Industry Trends:** Business developers must keep track of global economic trends, emerging technologies, and geopolitical shifts that can impact business strategies.
- ➢ **Invest in Continuous Learning:** Whether through professional certifications, business courses, or industry seminars, lifelong learning is a key differentiator.
- ➢ **Develop Cross-Industry Expertise:** While specialization is important, professionals who understand multiple industries can identify untapped opportunities and connect businesses across different sectors.

For Example: Business development professionals in the energy sector who are well-versed in renewable energy advancements, AI-driven predictive maintenance, and carbon emission regulations have a significant competitive advantage in today's sustainability-driven economy.

3. Build and Nurture Meaningful Relationships

Business development is fundamentally about people, trust, and partnerships. While products, pricing, and service offerings are important, the relationships you build define the longevity and quality of your career.

This necessitates a deliberate and strategic approach as follows:

- ➢ **Develop Authentic Professional Relationships:** Business is built on trust—clients and partners want to work with people they respect and rely on, not just companies with the best offerings.

> **Leverage Networking Opportunities:** Attend conferences, industry events, and professional meetups to expand your network and stay connected to decision-makers and influencers.

> **Focus on Relationship Longevity:** A strong business developer does not just close a deal and walk away. Consistent follow-ups, personalized engagement, and delivering on promises ensure repeat business and referrals.

For Example: Companies like Warren Buffett's Berkshire Hathaway have thrived for decades not just because of financial acumen but because of their strong long-term partnerships and trust-based business relationships.

4. Develop a Resilient and Problem-Solving Mindset

The world of business development is full of uncertainties, setbacks, and complex challenges. Whether it is facing rejections, managing difficult negotiations, or dealing with shifting market conditions, business development professionals must develop resilience and an adaptable mindset.

They must be prepared to:

> **Be Comfortable with Rejection:** In business development, not every deal will go through. Professionals must analyze failures, refine their approach, and move forward with confidence.

- ➤ **Adapt to Unexpected Challenges:** Market downturns, supply chain disruptions, and regulatory shifts are inevitable. The best business developers stay flexible and develop contingency plans.
- ➤ **Use First-Principles Thinking:** When traditional approaches fail, a business development professional should be able to break down challenges to their core components and find innovative solutions.

For Example: During the COVID-19 pandemic, many businesses had to change their strategies. Companies that quickly adapted their sales and engagement models to digital platforms survived, while those that waited, had to struggle.

5. Always See the Bigger Picture

Business development professionals must think beyond just company revenue targets. They should focus on value creation, industry impact, and sustainable business models.

Therefore, visionary business leaders must:

- ➤ **Understand how their role contributes to the Organization's Success:** Business development is not just about sales, but about positioning the company for long-term strategic growth.
- ➤ **Prioritize Ethical Business Practices:** The best business leaders build their careers on integrity,

ethical deal-making, and responsible business strategies.

> **Strive for Legacy over Short-Term Profits:** Professionals who think about their industry impact and business contributions often leave a lasting legacy in their field.

For Example: Industry Leaders like Elon Musk (Tesla, SpaceX) and Satya Nadella (Microsoft) don't just focus on profitability but on transforming industries, shaping future trends, and driving long-term innovation.

Final Thoughts: The Journey of a Business Development Professional

Becoming a successful business development professional is not just about learning a set of skills—it is about developing a mindset of adaptability, resilience, and long-term value creation. The most accomplished professionals in this field are those who continuously refine their approach, cultivate strong networks, and align their strategies with emerging industry trends.

For those entering the field or seeking to advance their careers, the key takeaways are:

> Think beyond individual deals—focus on long-term business value.
> Stay informed, continuously learn, and remain adaptable to market changes.
> Build genuine relationships—trust and partnerships drive business success.
> Embrace resilience—overcome challenges with a problem-solving mindset.

➢ See the bigger picture—align business development with innovation, impact, and sustainability.

With the right mindset, a commitment to learning, and a focus on building meaningful partnerships, aspiring business development professionals can position themselves for lasting success and leadership in the global business landscape.

The Future of Business Development in Energy Sector and Beyond

The business landscape is evolving faster than ever, and business development professionals must anticipate, adapt, and lead in this transformation. The energy sector, in particular, is undergoing a significant shift, driven by technological advancements, sustainability goals, regulatory changes, and global economic trends. While traditional business development strategies remain essential, the future will require a more data-driven, innovation-centric, and strategic approach to stay competitive.

Beyond the energy sector, business development as a function is also changing. The rise of AI, automation, geopolitical realignments, and digital commerce means that companies must redefine how they expand, negotiate deals, and enter new markets. Those who embrace the future, leverage technology, and build forward-thinking partnerships will lead the next wave of global business expansion.

Let's examine how these transformative forces are reshaping specific industries, starting with one of the most dramatically impacted sectors:

1. The Energy Sector: A Shift Toward Sustainability and Innovation

The energy industry is at the forefront of global transformation, with decarbonization, renewable energy adoption, and regulatory shifts driving new business development strategies. Companies must adapt to new technologies, changing consumer expectations, and government policies to remain competitive.

⇒ **Key Trends Shaping the Future of Energy Business Development**

1.1 The Rise of Renewable Energy and Clean Technologies

> ➢ The wave of energy transition is leading to shifting investments from fossil fuels to renewables such as solar, wind, hydrogen, and battery storage.
> ➢ Business development professionals associated with the Energy sector must identify opportunities in clean energy partnerships, government incentives, and carbon-reduction initiatives.

1.2 Decentralized Energy Markets and Smart Grids

- The traditional centralized energy production model is being replaced by decentralized grids that leverage microgrids, peer-to-peer energy trading, and AI-based optimization.
- Companies that adapt to digital energy solutions will gain a strategic advantage.

1.3 ESG (Environmental, Social, and Governance) as a Business Driver

- Governments and investors are prioritizing **ESG-compliant businesses**, impacting how companies secure funding and contracts.
- Business development professionals must align their strategies with sustainability and corporate responsibility initiatives.

1.4 AI and Automation in Energy Trading and Operations

- AI-driven predictive analytics are transforming energy trading, supply chain management, and risk assessment.
- Companies that integrate AI-based business intelligence tools will gain a significant competitive advantage.

For Example: Major oil companies like BP and Shell are focusing on Energy transition initiatives, investing in EV charging infrastructure, wind farms, and hydrogen production. Business development in these companies is no longer just about fossil fuels—it's about shaping the energy markets of the future.

2. The Role of Technology in the Future of Business Development

As industries become more digital-first, business development will increasingly depend on AI, big data, automation, and digital platforms. Companies that fail to embrace technology risk losing relevance in an increasingly competitive global economy.

⇒ **Key Technological Advancements Reshaping Business Development**

2.1 AI-Driven Market Research and Decision-Making

> ➤ AI can analyze market trends, customer behavior, and competitor strategies faster and more accurately than humans.
> ➤ Business development professionals who leverage AI for data-driven decision-making will outperform competitors.

2.2 Blockchain for Smart Contracts and Transparent Transactions

> ➤ Smart contracts can automate complex business agreements, ensuring secure, tamper-proof transactions.
> ➤ Companies engaged in global partnerships and trade agreements can reduce contract risks and inefficiencies through blockchain integration.

2.3 Virtual and Augmented Reality (VR/AR) for Client Engagement

> Virtual deal-making, digital site visits, and AI-powered presentations will transform client engagement and sales strategies.
> In the near future, Business developers will increasingly start using immersive technologies to pitch proposals and conduct cross-border negotiations.

2.4 The Expansion of Digital Commerce and Online B2B Marketplaces

> Traditional face-to-face deal-making is being supplemented (and in some cases replaced) by digital platforms.
> Companies must establish strong digital sales strategies and leverage e-commerce-driven B2B networks to expand globally.

For Example: Tesla disrupted the automotive industry by removing middlemen and selling directly through digital platforms, setting a precedent for B2B industries to move toward digital-first sales and strategic alliances.

3. The Global Business Landscape: Adapting to Geopolitical and Economic Shifts

Beyond technology and sustainability, global economic and geopolitical factors will play a defining role in business development strategies over the next decade.

$\Rightarrow$ **Key Global Trends Impacting Business Expansion and Deal-Making**

3.1 The Shift from Globalization to Regionalization

> Trade tensions, economic nationalism, and regional trade agreements are reshaping global supply chains.
> Companies must adapt to more localized sourcing and market expansion strategies.

3.2 The Rise of Emerging Markets

> Africa, Latin America, and Southeast Asia are experiencing rapid industrialization and growing consumer markets.
> Business developers must identify high-growth regions and tailor strategies for localized market entry.

3.3 Cybersecurity and Data Protection as a Competitive Advantage

> As businesses become more digital, cyber risks increase.
> Companies that prioritize secure digital infrastructure and compliance with international data regulations will have a market edge.

For Example: China's Belt and Road Initiative (BRI) is reshaping global trade routes, creating new opportunities for business developers in infrastructure, logistics, and investment partnerships.

4. What Business Development Professionals Must Do to Stay Ahead

Considering the rapidly evolving dynamics of the business landscapes, the business development professionals must:

4.1 Embrace AI and Digital Tools:

- ➢ Leverage AI for predictive analytics, deal structuring, and market intelligence.
- ➢ Adopt automation and CRM systems to streamline business operations.

4.2 Become Experts in Sustainability and ESG Compliance:

- Understand the evolving sustainability landscape and align business models with green energy initiatives and ethical sourcing.

4.3 Develop Geopolitical and Cultural Awareness:

- ➢ Learn how global regulations, trade policies, and regional business practices impact business expansion.
- ➢ Build cross-cultural communication and negotiation skills.

4.4 Adopt a Flexible and Crisis-Resilient Mindset:

> Develop adaptive business models that can change gears during economic downturns or industry disruptions.
> Prioritize partnerships and alliances that ensure long-term stability.

Final Thoughts: The Future of Business Development is About Adaptation and Innovation

The next decade of business development will be shaped by technology, sustainability, and geopolitical shifts. Companies and professionals who embrace change, innovate with digital tools, and align with emerging global trends will be at the forefront of business expansion and strategic growth.

Business development is no longer just about finding new markets—it is about redefining how companies operate, engage with customers, and build long-term value in an interconnected global economy.

For those willing to adapt, learn, and think strategically, the future holds limitless opportunities in energy, technology, and beyond.

Chapter 11: Appendices

This section provides valuable resources for business development professionals, including templates, practical tools, and industry terminology that can aid in strategic planning, market analysis, and execution. These appendices serve as a quick reference guide to help professionals implement the concepts discussed throughout the book.

Templates for Business Development Plans

A well-structured business development plan serves as a blueprint for growth, outlining strategies, target markets, resource allocation, and execution timelines. Below is a comprehensive template to guide professionals in crafting an effective business development strategy.

⇒ **Business Development Plan Template**

A. Executive Summary

> Brief overview of business goals and market opportunities.
> Summary of key strategies and expected outcomes.

B. Market Analysis

> **Target Market Segments**: Define primary and secondary markets.

> **Competitive Landscape**: SWOT analysis of competitors.
> **Industry Trends**: Market drivers, regulatory factors, and emerging technologies.

C. Business Development Strategy

> **Lead Generation & Client Acquisition**: Key channels and outreach methods.
> **Strategic Partnerships**: Potential alliances and industry collaborations.
> **Expansion Plan**: Geographic and sector-based growth strategies.

D. Financial Projections & Budgeting

> **Revenue Forecasts**: 3-5 year growth projections.
> **Investment Needs**: Capital requirements and funding sources.
> **Cost Analysis**: Operational expenses and risk mitigation planning.

E. Key Performance Indicators (KPIs)

> Revenue Growth Rate

> Customer Acquisition Cost (CAC)
> Client Retention Metrics
> ROI on Business Development Initiatives

F. Risk Management & Contingency Planning

  - ➢ Identification of potential risks (economic, political, technological).
  - ➢ Risk mitigation strategies and crisis response planning.

G. Implementation Timeline & Milestones

  - ➢ Short-Term Goals (0-6 months)
  - ➢ Mid-Term Goals (6-18 months)
  - ➢ Long-Term Goals (18+ months)

Practical Tools for Market Research and Analysis

Business development requires data-driven decision-making, and the right tools can provide valuable insights into market conditions, competition, and consumer trends. Below are some of the most effective tools for conducting market research and analysis.

⇒ **Market Research Tools**

1. Google Trends

  - ➢ Identifies search patterns and consumer interest in specific topics.
  - ➢ Useful for tracking industry trends over time.

2. Statista

  - ➢ Provides industry reports, market data, and sector-specific analysis.

> Helps in benchmarking company performance against market averages.

3. IBISWorld

> Comprehensive reports on industry trends, key players, and emerging risks.
> Ideal for sector-specific business development planning.

4. Crunchbase & LinkedIn Sales Navigator

> Helps identify potential partners, investors, and competitors.
> Provides insights into corporate growth and funding trends.

⇒ **Competitive Analysis & Benchmarking Tools**

1. SWOT Analysis Framework

> **Strengths:** What gives your business a competitive edge?
> **Weaknesses:** What are the operational or market limitations?
> **Opportunities:** Where are the gaps in the market?
> **Threats:** What risks or industry shifts could impact growth?

2. Porter's Five Forces Analysis

- ➢ Evaluates the competitive intensity and attractiveness of a market.
- ➢ **Key Forces:** Supplier power, buyer power, competitive rivalry, threat of new entrants, threat of substitutes.

3. P.E.S.T.E.L. Analysis

- ➢ **Political:** Government policies, trade regulations.
- ➢ **Economic:** Market trends, currency fluctuations, inflation.
- ➢ **Social:** Consumer behavior, cultural shifts.
- ➢ **Technological:** Innovations, AI, automation impact.
- ➢ **Environmental:** Sustainability regulations, carbon footprint mandates.
- ➢ **Legal:** Compliance, industry-specific legal requirements.

⇒ Financial & Investment Analysis Tools

1. Bloomberg Terminal

- ➢ Industry-leading financial data, economic reports, and investment insights.
- ➢ Helps in evaluating market conditions before expanding operations.

2. Yahoo Finance & Morningstar

- ➢ Tracks stock performance, investor sentiment, and corporate valuations.
- ➢ Useful for understanding investor trends in key industries.

3. AI-Powered Market Forecasting Tools

> ➤ Tools like **IBM Watson Analytics, Tableau, and Power BI** help analyze large datasets for market predictions.
> ➤ Ideal for businesses developing long-term business expansion strategies.

Glossary of Industry Terms

This glossary provides definitions for key business development and market strategy terms, serving as a quick reference guide for professionals.

⇒ Business Development Terms

1. **B2B (Business-to-Business)** – Transactions between businesses rather than consumers.
2. **B2C (Business-to-Consumer)** – Companies selling directly to individual consumers.
3. **Lead Generation** – The process of identifying potential customers and nurturing them into prospects.
4. **Conversion Rate** – The percentage of leads that convert into actual customers.
5. **Customer Lifetime Value (CLV)** – The total projected revenue from a single customer over the course of their relationship with a business.
6. **Key Performance Indicators (KPIs)** – Metrics used to measure the success of business development efforts (e.g., revenue growth, lead conversion rates).

7. **Go-to-Market (GTM) Strategy** – A business development roadmap for launching a product or expanding into new markets.
8. **Stakeholder Engagement** – The process of building and maintaining relationships with key business partners, clients, and regulatory bodies.

⇒ Market Strategy and Financial Terms

1. **Market Segmentation** – Dividing a market into specific groups based on demographics, behavior, or industry needs.
2. **Competitive Positioning** – How a company differentiates itself in the market relative to competitors.
3. **Return on Investment (ROI)** – A measure of profitability in relation to investment costs.
4. **Equity Stake** – The percentage of ownership a company holds in a joint venture or partnership.
5. **Capital Expenditure (CAPEX) vs. Operational Expenditure (OPEX)**
   - ➢ **CAPEX** refers to long-term investments (infrastructure, assets, equipment).
   - ➢ **OPEX** refers to day-to-day operational costs (payroll, maintenance, marketing).
6. **Merger & Acquisition (M&A)** – The process of combining two or more companies for strategic growth.
7. **Due Diligence** – The research and risk assessment process before finalizing a business deal.

⇒ **Business Development and Market Expansion Terms**

1. **Business Development Pipeline** – A structured process for tracking potential clients, partnerships, and sales opportunities from initial contact to deal closure.
2. **Value Proposition** – A clear statement that explains why a client should choose a business over its competitors, highlighting unique benefits and solutions offered.
3. **Sales Funnel** – The process of converting prospects into paying customers, typically structured in 4 stages: Awareness → Interest → Decision → Action.
4. **Account-Based Marketing (ABM)** – A highly targeted B2B marketing strategy where businesses personalize outreach efforts to specific high-value accounts.
5. **Customer Acquisition Cost (CAC)** – The total cost required to acquire a new customer, including marketing, sales, and onboarding expenses.
6. **Churn Rate** – The percentage of customers lost over a specific period, indicating customer retention and business stability.
7. **Cross-Selling and Upselling** – Strategies used to increase customer lifetime value (CLV):

> **Cross-selling** involves selling related products or services to an existing customer.

> **Upselling** encourages customers to purchase a higher-end product or upgrade their service plan.

8. **Brand Equity** – The perceived value and reputation of a brand, influencing customer loyalty and market competitiveness.

9. **Market Entry Strategy** – A structured plan for expanding into a new geographic or industry-specific market, including direct investment, joint ventures, and partnerships.

10. **Omnichannel Strategy** – A business approach that integrates multiple sales and communication channels (online, in-person, mobile, and social media) for a seamless customer experience.

11. **White Labeling** – A business model where one company produces a product or service that another company rebrands and sells as its own.

12. **Franchising Model** – A market expansion strategy where a business allows external partners to operate under its brand name in exchange for licensing fees and royalties.

⇒ **Financial and Investment Terms**

1. **Market Capitalization (Market Cap)** – The total value of a company's outstanding shares,

used to determine its size and investment attractiveness.

2. **EBITDA (Earnings Before Interest, Taxes, Depreciation, and Amortization)** – A financial metric that evaluates a company's profitability before accounting for financial obligations and non-cash expenses.

3. **Gross Margin vs. Net Margin** –
   - **Gross Margin**: Revenue minus the direct cost of goods sold (COGS), representing profitability before operational expenses.
   - **Net Margin**: The final profit after all expenses, taxes, and operating costs are deducted from revenue.

4. **Burn Rate** – The rate at which a company is spending its available cash reserves, often used in startups and investment analysis.

5. **Liquidity Ratio** – A financial measure that assesses a company's ability to cover short-term liabilities with its available assets.

6. **Debt-to-Equity Ratio** – A financial indicator that evaluates a company's financial leverage by comparing its debt levels to shareholder equity.

7. **Capital Efficiency** – A measure of how effectively a business utilizes financial and operational resources to generate profits.

8. **Letter of Credit (LC)** – A financial instrument used in international trade where a bank guarantees that a buyer's payment to a seller will be received on time.

9. **Convertible Notes** – A form of short-term debt that converts into equity in a company, commonly used in early-stage startup funding.
10. **Private Equity (PE) vs. Venture Capital (VC)** –
    - ➢ **Private Equity**: Investment in **mature companies** with growth potential, often involving ownership restructuring.
    - ➢ **Venture Capital**: Investment in **early-stage startups** with high growth potential but higher risk.
11. **Exit Strategy** – A planned approach for business owners or investors to liquidate their stake in a company, often through mergers, acquisitions, or IPOs.

⇒ **Strategic Planning and Risk Management Terms**

1. **Blue Ocean Strategy** – A business approach that creates uncontested market space by offering unique, high-value products or services, reducing direct competition.
2. **First-Mover Advantage** – The competitive benefit a company gains by entering a new market or launching an innovative product before competitors.
3. **Disruptive Innovation** – A new technology or business model that significantly alters an industry, making traditional offerings obsolete.

4. **Scenario Planning** – A strategic forecasting technique that models different future market conditions and business responses.
5. **Business Continuity Plan (BCP)** – A risk management strategy that ensures critical business operations continue uninterrupted during crises, such as supply chain disruptions or economic downturns.
6. **Political Risk Analysis** – The process of assessing potential regulatory, trade, and geopolitical risks that could impact business operations.
7. **Cyber Risk Management** – The implementation of data security, compliance protocols, and digital protection measures to prevent financial and reputational losses.
8. **Economic Moat** – A company's competitive advantage that protects it from market threats, such as strong brand identity, exclusive technology, or economies of scale.
9. **Joint Venture vs. Strategic Alliance:**

   - **Joint Venture**: A formal agreement where two companies create a new business entity for shared interests.
   - **Strategic Alliance**: A loose collaboration where companies maintain independence but work together on specific projects.

10. **Vertical vs. Horizontal Integration:**

> **Vertical Integration**: A company expands into different stages of its supply chain (e.g., a manufacturer acquiring a raw materials supplier).

> **Horizontal Integration**: A company acquires competitors to expand market share (e.g., a beverage company acquiring another soft drink brand).

11. **Corporate Governance** – The system of rules, practices, and processes that direct a company's operations and decision-making, ensuring transparency and accountability.

⇒ **Digital Business and Emerging Technology Terms**

1. **Artificial Intelligence (AI) in Business Development** – AI tools that automate data analysis, customer engagement, and market predictions to improve business expansion strategies.

2. **Internet of Things (IoT) in Industry** – The use of connected devices and real-time data collection to enhance operational efficiency in manufacturing, logistics, and retail.

3. **FinTech (Financial Technology)** – The integration of AI, blockchain, and digital banking solutions into financial services to optimize payments, lending, and investment processes.

4. **Metaverse and Virtual Business Engagement** – The emerging use of virtual reality (VR) and augmented reality (AR) for remote business meetings, training, and customer interactions.

5. **Big Data Analytics in Market Research** – The process of using large-scale data sets and AI-driven insights to identify customer behaviors, trends, and business opportunities.

6. **Digital Twin Technology** – A virtual simulation of real-world business processes, supply chains, or industrial operations, enabling businesses to test strategies before implementation.

Final Thoughts: A Toolkit for Business Development Success

These templates, tools, and industry insights are designed to help business development professionals navigate challenges, optimize decision-making, and craft winning strategies.

By applying these frameworks, analysis tools, and best practices, professionals can maximize market opportunities, drive revenue growth, and establish sustainable business relationships in an increasingly competitive global economy.

About the Author

 Vikram Anand is a seasoned International Business Development leader with over 20 years of experience in the global Oil & Gas, Energy, Infrastructure, and Consulting sectors. He specializes in driving market expansion strategies, forging high-value partnerships, and executing complex projects across international markets. His expertise spans across business strategy development, financial evaluation, cost optimization, and leveraging Generative AI for strategic business insights.

As an International Business Development Professional, Vikram has led multi-million-dollar projects, successfully negotiated high-stakes contracts, and spearheaded business growth initiatives in diverse geographies. His leadership in market research, stakeholder engagement, and crisis management has contributed to the success of several large-scale ventures.

A passionate advocate for AI-driven business transformation, Vikram blends traditional business acumen with emerging technologies to optimize decision-making and enhance operational efficiency.

This practical guide, **Beyond Borders: Winning Strategies for International Business**, offers practical frameworks, real-world case studies, and actionable insights for professionals looking to master the complexities of business development, strategic alliances, and global expansion.